The Curmudgeon Epistles

Grievances of a Bitter Soul

Tom Luddecke

Printed in the United States of America

Cover design by Paper & Sage Design
Front cover illustration by Dennis Cox
Formatting by Polgarus Studio

First Printing: April, 2016
ISBN-13: 978-1530710447
ISBN-10: 1530710448
10 9 8 7 6 5 4 3 2 1

To everyone who has shown the patience in enduring my complaints and who have the ulcers to prove it. This especially includes my family and a few close friends who understand me and accept the fact that this is who I am, and yet, still hate me for it. I could not have done this without you. Lacking a sympathetic ear, I would be much like that toppling tree in the forest with no one around to hear it fall.

And

To Nancy, who I know I embarrass to no end with my idiosyncrasies.

*I personally believe we developed language
because of our deep inner need to complain.*

- Jane Wagner

The Search for Signs of Intelligent Life in the Universe

Disclaimer

Warning: The ensuing pages contain strong language, some verbal violence, but thankfully, no nudity or sexual situations that are readily identifiable. It is intended for mature audiences only. Viewer discretion is advised.

With that formality attended to, the following additional disclaimers should be noted.

Do not read this book if you:

- Believe you currently reside on a plane of spiritual enlightenment, balance, and peace, or are about to achieve such a plane. Wait…I've changed my mind on this one. If you do indeed exist in such a state of mind, then you should most definitely read this book and join the rest of us on the same playing field of angst, disappointment, and unfulfilled dreams.
- Are or were a member in organizations such as the Peace Corps, Red Cross, Salvation Army, or any religious order which features hope and forgiveness as the centerpieces of its doctrine, because you will find none of that namby-pamby shit within these pages. So move on.
- Have even a smidgen of unabated faith in humankind.
- Have a habit, on occasion, of turning the other cheek.

- Belong to a nature conservatory, ASPCA chapter, any charity, or are under consideration for canonization.
- Truly believe in unicorns and that they poop rainbows.

This should leave only two groups of people who should read this book. In the first group, we have folks like me, who complain incessantly about the second group, which is made up of all the rest of you people responsible for committing those acts of social improprieties, discourteous deeds of public malfeasance, and the aggrandizement of selfish intentions, all of which, serve to raise the hackles of curmudgeons, cranks, and grumps everywhere.

I would like to believe that if those people did read this book, then it just might change their outrageous behavior, which is the cause of our misery. In truth, I do not think you even recognize such behavior as being exceedingly in the wrong. Then again, if by chance, you truly are cognizant of your irritating, arrogant, and selfish actions, but you just don't give a camel's hump about it, you might deserve everything you get from this point on.

Preface

In case you failed to read or heed the previous disclaimers, I'll give you one last warning. If you claim to be one of those people who wake up each morning with a smile on your face and leap out of bed while whistling a happy tune, then you need read no further. If you're always looking on the bright side of things or see the glass half-full, you don't belong here. If you are forever being described as having a sunny disposition, you should leave…now.

Oh, but before you go, I want you to know one thing. I do not believe people like you, in fact, truly exist. You are as genuine as the Tooth Fairy, Easter Bunny, or that jolly old elf himself. Yet, if you still insist you are indeed such a Pollyanna, then please email me your address, because I will come and sit by your bed all night—not in that creepy sort of way—but to be there when you awake. I want to witness for myself that daybreak smile of which you so boast. Now, if I'm wrong, and you are indeed wearing said smirk upon arising, then I will be there to slap it right off that cherubic face of yours before the cock crows.

The point is that no one lives with a perpetual sunny disposition. That's just what the public sees. If truth were told, we all have our good natures jerked around at one time or another. That's okay. Even Santa scribbles a few names on the debit side of the ledger every now and then. Therefore, if you are one of those so-called, benevolent beings, don't be so afraid of a few negative feelings that might come along periodically. Trust me; this is a natural occurrence for the rest of us. Why, it's even healthy occasionally to vent at someone or something that has aggrieved you in some way. I'm sure there must be some medical study that backs me up on this. As humans, we have a basic need to grouse from time to time, and for some of us, this happens more often…okay, much more often.

It is for these people that this book is intended and dedicated. They understand. They know. It's not because we possess a nasty temperament, see the glass half-empty, or look on the negative side of things. We grumble, piss and moan because it makes us feel better. We view it as an advocacy of our moral composition—judge others as we would be judged, if you will—only a little stricter on the others.

Think of us as the defenders of those of you who wear those rose-colored spectacles. For it is clear that you do not or cannot see the habitual idiocies of others, along with the outrageous, selfish acts perpetrated against you. Rest assured, we have your backs. Sometimes our gripes might actually be heeded, and the source of our irritation alleviated. This means there will be one less situation to tempt you from your lofty perches.

Sadly, more often than not, our grievances fall on the deaf ears of people so self-absorbed, they will not change either themselves or the annoying things they do. Yet, we are a resilient lot and we will continue to carp, because at the end of the day, we go to bed with smiles on our faces, content we have done our part to right the world. Then, we arise each morning with scowls in place to welcome a crappy new day. We do this because we are the curmudgeons. Hear us roar.

P.S. Now, this time I really mean it. Any humanist still on board this train wreck needs to get off right now. Go on…before I begin. Just remember, if you stay, you have been warned.

Acknowledgements

First, I would like to acknowledge my pens, paper, computer, thesaurus, dictionary, and the internet. The support you provided was invaluable, although somewhat mundane. Finally, as a gesture of irony, I must reluctantly recognize all those assholes that provided the fodder for my cannon. May you one day fall prey to your own medicine and finally get it.

Contents

Preface ix

Acknowledgements xiii

Introduction 1

The Pet Peeves 9

    A Few to Start With 11

    What's in a Name? 20

    Misery Loves Company 22

    You Don't Say 24

    Undercover Activity 26

    And a Few to End With 30

The Complaints 35

    You Are No Longer Free to Move about the Cabin .. 37

    This Space: *Not for Sale* 44

    With Apologies to Hervé Villechaize 48

    A Loss of Innocence 52

    Car Sickness 55

    Parking Lot Drones 60

    Beasts of Burden 65

    The Worst of the Bunch 68

The Rants 73

    Weather or Not.. 75

    Minimum Rage... 84

    # 1984... 93

    Surviving the Cure 101

    Wildlife Strife.. 108

    The Game of Greed 124

    Driving Me Crazy 139

The Final Blessing....................................... 153

Introduction

Hello, my name is Tom, and I am a curmudgeon. This is usually the part of the meeting where you all respond, "Hello, Tom." However, this is not an intervention, but rather an admittance on my part to being somewhat cantankerous in nature. I come by this naturally, that is, by way of genetics. I'm guessing that's how most curmudgeonliness develops. In my case, I believe the chromosome for this trait was passed down to me from the paternal branches of the tree. Although, I suppose it's possible some people may be turned on to this path due to environmental factors, such as the number of idiots per square neighborhood one lives in, or perhaps the amount of exposure to the blusters and rants of sourpusses during impressionable years. However, I genuinely believe it is more likely that we are born this way.

For us curmudgeons, the aging process is what hones our surly skills. Along our evolutionary progression, there exists earlier stages through which we must pass in order to one day attain the rank of curmudgeon. These levels would include the whiner, griper, grump, crank, and finally, full-blown curmudgeon-status itself. For most of us, this is where the process usually ends. Unfortunately, a few individuals will continue further down this bleak path, eventually reaching a place of darkness and animosity. This is where the misanthrope resides.

I am not a misanthrope. A misanthrope hates and distrusts

humankind. This, I can assure you, I do not do. If this book was entitled, *The Misanthrope Epistles*, it might begin something like this:

> *Human beings are simply blobs of electrified protoplasm and most times their wiring misfires, doesn't fire at all, or is just not connected in the right way. When this occurs, anything can and usually does happen. You just don't want to be anywhere in the vicinity when it does.*

> *I have no tolerance for the actions of humanity. This would include both the physical and mental productions it might manifest. As a whole, humans are incessantly inane, inapt, and inept. The primary reason for this is due to their brains being the size of Tic Tacs. For those of you morons reading this sometime in the future—if you can indeed read at all—Tic Tacs were tiny oblong breath mints used by these cretins to mask the terrible smell caused by the cranial exhaust emitted by their immature brain stumps.*

Okay…you get the idea—a real case of bitterness going on there. As I said, I'm not that far off the charts and I just ask that you remember this while reading my criticisms in this book. Just realize these would have gone on a much more malevolent trip under the pen of a misanthrope.

The *Merriam-Webster Online Dictionary* defines a curmudgeon as "a person (especially an old man) who is easily annoyed and who complains." This description clearly identifies two essential characteristics that semantically differentiate this type of person from another of a similar ilk known as the *crank*. The crank is defined by the same source as "a person who is often angry or easily annoyed." Now, lest you think this sounds strikingly similar to the description of the first testy individual, you would be only partially right. Although both characters are defined as being quick with the temper, the dictionary does not represent them as being synonymous. One difference is that a curmudgeon is nearly always described as being an old man. This is further supported in Merriam-Webster's second definition of a curmudgeon as "a crusty, ill-tempered, and usually old man." While the adjectives used to describe these grousers are varied (crusty, ill tempered, irascible, churlish, surly, grumpy, or cantankerous), almost all of them agree to a tome on the old man part. A crank, meanwhile, appears not to be age-defined.

The second dissimilarity is that while both of these individuals are easily annoyed and angered, it is the curmudgeon who complains discordantly about it, or at least, more frequently. Perhaps a simple comparison would better illustrate this distinction.

You're a crank if the actions of someone or something cause you to scowl or shake your head in displeasure. You know you're a curmudgeon when you perceive these actions to be intentional, view them in the worst possible light, and then vociferously voice your disapproval. You know you are a misanthrope—just to create a benchmark here—when you hate everyone and everything before they do or say anything at all.

As I admit to being a curmudgeon, it is from this viewpoint these epistles have been written. However, before getting to my gripes and complaints, I would like to go on a minor offensive for just a moment. I don't want it inferred in any manner that we curmudgeons, or even cranks, for that matter, are always full of vitriolic sentiments. Nothing could be further from the truth. In fact, most of the time, we are pleasant, productive people, whom you would never even suspect harbored extreme sensitivity to social gaffes and irritating behaviors; that is, until we are provoked into action by some idiotic situation, and even then, you might deem our verbal complaints in a positive fashion and even warranted. Look at it as our way of alerting the rest of the world to the bonehead moves of inconsiderate jerks. We view ourselves as providing a valuable social service. Think of us as the moral compasses or barometers of societal behavior. Moreover, since by definition, curmudgeons are old men, then over the span of our long lives we have been exposed to a multitude of incidents of thoughtless acts of human unkindness, inconsideration, and selfishness. This experience has trained us to become receptive to the foibles of human deportment.

This book is divided into three sections. The first and shorter section will deal with my secondary gripes, which are more personal in their offensiveness and are generally referred to as pet peeves. The second part lists my complaints, and while these can still be of a personal nature, they usually also enjoy wider recognition as being inappropriate in their moral and ethical appearance. The last and longest component of the book consists of my invectives against more perturbing issues, which I tend to go on about on a more regular basis. It is here that I will ask for your forgiveness in advance if I tend to perseverate too much.

To those amazing people who don't "sweat the small stuff" as they go through life, I am sure you will consider these rants and those of my colleagues as being trivial in nature and destined to lead us into a life full of ulcers and stress-related maladies. However, in our defense, I present the argument that it is this same small stuff, which we encounter each day that eventually adds up to the big stuff that will set even you, the even-keeled ones, on the path to medicated depression and expensive analysis, having suppressed the small stuff warnings all your lives. Some of you may bury this stuff so deeply that your psychiatrist will need to take on the role of an archeologist just to uncover those hidden Easter eggs.

I guess what I'm trying to say is that it might behoove you to heed our complaints about these issues you may view as being so inconsequential. As malcontents, we are not unlike the canaries in the coalmines. Therefore, on behalf of curmudgeons everywhere, I say, you're welcome.

To the layperson, who only on occasion gripes about things, the following terms are often used interchangeably. That's understandable due to the infrequency of their use. However, to us, the connoisseurs of complaints, each term represents its own distinct class of umbrage and is therefore used accordingly.

We separate our criticisms into three main categories: pet peeves, complaints, and rants. So here, my dear, emotionally unflappable, roll-with-the-punches, turn-the-other-cheek non-professionals, are the descriptions of each cavil in the order of their level of irritation from least to most.

The Pet Peeve

This minor grouse annoys and often makes us resentful toward the offending person or thing. Sometimes referred to as a gripe, it is often more specific in nature than the other two categories and provides us with a source of continual aggravation. Examples might include drivers who don't use their turn signals, or people who park on your street and close enough to your driveway, so that it becomes difficult to back out.

Please, do not misunderstand me in thinking these are petty concerns. Some of these can be downright infuriating, but the effect doesn't last as long as the other two types listed below. Our crankiness usually dissipates shortly after the occurrence of the offending peeve. Unfortunately, this peace will only last until the next appearance of the provoking incident—hence, the continual annoyance aspect of this type of gripe. In such cases, grumbling is normally kept to a minimum.

The Complaint

This grievance arises as a result of some cause of discontent, grief, or pain. It can be either of short duration or of lengthy tenure. It is oftentimes accompanied by a feeling that some social injustice has been visited upon us. The degree of its irritation in terms of either time span or intensity is what differentiates it from the pet peeve. Carping here, can go on for longer periods of time and will often become bothersome to anyone around its distribution.

The Rant

This is often referred to as a diatribe, tirade, or verbal attack. It is typically more verbose than the others. Although it can be oral in nature, many times it is presented as a written declaration. It is often the result of a longstanding, egregious issue, at times prompting us to declaim in op-ed pieces or letters to the editor, with our characteristically brash, vehement, and almost always, extravagant manner.

So, let this serve as one last warning to those people with sunny dispositions and charitable forbearances who are uncomfortable in the company of whiners, grousers, and malcontents. Do not enter these pages of caustic condemnations. Turn away now and go kiss a butterfly or whatever else it is you do with your good nature and forever preserve your soul from being compromised.

Now, let us begin.

The Pet Peeves

I've decided to begin each section with a quotation befitting the grievance. For this first one, it's a reader's choice.

<u>G-rated Quote</u>
I don't have pet peeves; I have whole kennels of irritation.
- Whoopi Goldberg

<u>R-rated Quote</u>
I don't have pet peeves—I have major psychotic fucking hatreds!
- George Carlin

Everybody has them. It's just that we curmudgeons tend to be more vocal when it comes to them. Obviously, we tend to have more pet peeves than the average person does, simply because we are so adept at recognizing them.

While the effect of a pet peeve might only warrant a minor annoyance due to the brevity of duration at the time of its appearance, it is the longevity of its occurrences, which makes it so maddening. Pet peeves continually happen over and over and over again.

A Few to Start With

Epistle to the Tormentors

First, I would like to offer a few thoughts concerning pet peeves. Frankly, I'm at a loss to explain why these annoyances are described using adjectives such as *pet* or *favorite*. It's clearly an oxymoronic phrase, like saying b*eloved bigotries* or something along those lines. Abhorrent aggravations would be a more accurate description, but I guess you work with what you've been given.

In compiling this section, I discovered that most of my pet peeves involved people in some way. I'm assuming this is probably true for my fellow curmudgeons as well. This makes sense given that, what really cheeses you off—despite what the misanthrope may think—is the fact that human beings do have highly developed brain matter and when they do commit to an act of idiocy, you know they have the ability to do otherwise, but instead choose not to. Even in those instances when my gripe concerns an inanimate object, there is by and large, some human participation. The only examples I can think of, off the top of my head, in which people bear no responsibility are those relating to nature. Even then, folks seem determined, intentionally or not, to become involved.

I believe the reason people are at the heart of most of these disconcerting irritations is due to their unbridled selfishness, lack of civility, laziness, self-absorption, or blatant ignorance. After all, a little common sense and courtesy, and most of these nuisances go away. But, therein lies the rub, my friends. For you see, most curmudgeons recognize that our society today isn't built that way. Outside of family and a few friends, people are drawing further apart from each other, providing less real interpersonal contact to develop those redeeming social skills, which would prevent most personal pet peeves from even occurring. Whether the blame falls on current technology or the increasingly demanding lives of humans, the end result is that people have become more distant and distracted, and consequently further removed from the sensitive treatment of their fellow beings.

It's not that people didn't piss each other off in the past. Burr and Hamilton, Stalin and Trotsky, Hatfields and McCoys, are just to name a few historical examples. And there were, of course, more than enough wars to substantiate this fact further. At the same time though, there existed an acknowledged code of personal conduct on how to behave when dealing with your neighbors.

Even as late as the 1960s, there were the Emily Posts to remind us of the proper way to act in different social circumstances. Today, many of those manners appear to be lost. Meanwhile, the churlish demeanors exhibited by many of our so-called "role models," are splashed all over the media landscape and are unfortunately viewed by many as authorization to emulate the same boorish conduct.

Please don't misread me. There are still plenty of decent people around today, but sadly, this population appears to be declining. And as bad manners increase, the number of curmudgeons grows larger in response to the burgeoning crisis.

At this point, I would like to start with only a short list of my personal pet peeves, so as not to overwhelm you from the get-go. While I may not be delving as deeply into these as I will with the ones that follow, this doesn't mean I take them any less seriously. They can be as vexing to me as the others are, still causing palpitations to my black heart.

Finally, I know that many of you may view these peeves as trivial or even petty, but I really don't care because these are my own. Go make your own inventory if it bothers you that much. Then you can put me at the top of your list. That's what I would do if you complained about mine. In fact…let's go ahead and do just that.

Pet Peeve #1: *Jerks*
Idiots who get upset over someone else's petty shit that gets them upset (see above).

Pet Peeve #2: *F***ing Tinted Windows*
Seriously? Just what are you people doing in your vehicles that is so secretive, nasty, or illegal that you need to hide it while driving? When I'm parked next to you, those windows make it impossible to view oncoming traffic as I attempt to leave my space. And don't give me that, "I don't want anyone to see that I have a child with me," or "I have merchandise that might tempt someone to break into my car to steal." Spoiler alert! Tinted glass as such, automatically screams your car might be worth a look-see because of what it might be hiding. And if you don't have anything of value inside…oh, well…insurance might cover that smash and no-grab debris.

Also, don't worry about giving away you have a Baby on Board, because that cute, little bumper sticker on your tinted window already advertises this fact. And that even smarmier decal, displaying those endearing stick figures of your family, not only exposes them, but any pets you chose to include as well. Oh, and by the way—just so you know—if you own a minivan it is a redundancy to place one of these obnoxious stickers on your window, as it is implicit in the ownership of that vehicle.

Pet Peeve #3: *Oblivious Pedestrians*
There are two issues here. The first one deals with those walkers whom I call the Sightseers. Habitats such as sidewalks and store aisles are rife with those creatures. They will be the ones moving in a leisurely crawl, scanning in all directions, perhaps for some object that will hopefully remind them of where they were going or what they came in to buy. It can be very difficult to get around these "tourists," not only because they tend to stroll in the middle of the sidewalk or aisle, but they can unexpectedly start utilizing a weaving maneuver, which often then places their pokiness directly in front of your attempt at circumvention.

The second breed of inconsiderate walkers would be those pedestrians who tend to migrate as a flock on sidewalks. Instead of politely consolidating their promenade into a column of two by twos, they continue to stretch themselves across the entire walkway, blocking any faster moving pedestrians who might be behind them. If those pavement hogs are coming towards you, there is no way they are going to break their BFF chain in order to let you pass in your own designated right hand lane. You are then forced to step off the curb and into the road, while they continue on past, chattering away, oblivious to your existence or the fact they have just jettisoned a fellow human being into the road and into possible harm's way. My wife has become so infuriated with this lack of civility that she now refuses to step aside from her own rightful passage. She will stop motionless in their path like a boulder against an onrushing wave. Then the flock has to break rank to get by or walk right into her. Either way, this forces them—at least temporarily—to acknowledge her presence either consciously or subconsciously. You go, girl!

Oh, and while I'm at it, those of you who find it impossible to walk from here to there without interacting with your cell phone, need to stop and smell the roses. Come up for air and survey your surroundings if only to confirm that a runaway car isn't bearing down on you or that an open manhole doesn't await your next distracted step. Come to think about it; who am I to intervene with Darwinism?

Pet Peeve #4: *Shipping and Handling Charges*

If you ask me, this should be more appropriately labeled as shipping and *manhandling*. I understand the shipping piece, but it's the handling part that I'm having issues with. This has to be one of the biggest scams going on in the mail retail business sector. It's right up there with those extended warranties, and bait and switch tactics. Anyway, just what the hell constitutes handling? Am I being charged for someone fetching my ordered item and then packaging it in the box? Isn't that the job of someone in the company, and why am I paying for that and not the owner? Let's call this what it really is, a plain and simple, blatant markup sham. You've purchased what sounded like a great deal on a cigar-shaped item that dispenses melted butter, but are then smacked with outrageous handling charges in order to jack up company profits. For this type of charge, I expect my order to be handled with goatskin gloves and gift wrapped in Tiffany blue.

The extreme absurdity of this type of charade is even more clearly evidenced when buying event tickets online. Even though they are sending you an e-ticket through the internet, they will still charge a handling fee, despite the fact that you are the one clicking and printing the ticket.

Of course, the real giveaway to these kinds of swindles is when you are offered *not just one, but TWO cases of bacon-flavored return-address labels for one low price*. All you need to do, of course, is pay separate shipping and handling charges on the second item. Screw you, buddy! Here's a corporate suggestion box stuffer for you—how about having the "handler" grab two off the shelf while he's at it and throw them in one box? There, that peeve has been handled!

Pet Peeve #5: *Discarded Cigarette Butts*
If they're not good enough for you to keep, what makes you think we want them? It's bad enough that you even have this disgusting habit, but then you go and compound its contemptibility by making the world your personal ashtray. On the one hand, I'm delighted car manufacturers have removed ashtrays from their vehicles, if only to stop the one-percenters from joking about a full ashtray as being their excuse for buying a new car. Yet now, with no receptacles for their remains, these smokestacks are forced to flick ash and butts out their car

windows. Previously, at least you would find the discarded filters dumped from an ashtray in one neat pile on the road, usually at a stoplight or sign. Now, these litterbugs are strewing them all over the terrain. Buttheads.

Pet Peeve #6: *Turn Signals—and no…I don't know what you're thinking.*
Believe it or not, every car comes standard with this handy lever on the left side of the steering column. It resides there for a reason, and despite apparent belief, the use of this turn signal is not optional. It actually alerts your fellow motorists of your intention of going this way or that way.

And while I'm at it…

Pet Peeve #7: *Other Drivers Who Obviously Received Their Licenses Along with Their Costco Memberships.*
Pretty much everyone and everything they do on the road gnarls the tar out of me. In fact, there is simply too much to write about in this small piece. So please torment yourselves by reading my full indignation on this subject under the titles, *Misery Loves Company* and *Driving Me Crazy*.

Pet Peeve # 8: *Political Correctness*
If by now, and for some incomprehensible reason, you can't hazard a guess on where I stand on this baby, then someone hasn't been paying attention or is reading in snippets just before falling asleep in bed and losing any continuity of this book's subject matter, thus forfeiting any chance of interpretive or applied comprehension of this material.

Look…I'm assuming we're all grownups here. Most of us should be smart enough to distinguish what is meant as derision, and what is meant for emphasis. There's being sensitive and then there's being overly sensitive, or as I like to think of it—as having a dainty, easily-offended threshold. Self-censoring words or descriptions which are not intended to be offensive is turning our language blasé and boring—speech that is stifled and stilted, and writing that is blanched.

As it pertains to word choice and usage, intent is the key aspect here. Laziness in interpreting this attribute is what generally brings the PC card into play. We need to grow up and use our words without having to look over our shoulders to see if some philistine is offended for misinterpreting our implication. If I call something a horse, and I mean a horse and not an ass, then it should stand without criticism. Things are what they are. That's all there is to say here.

Pet Peeve #9: *False Alarmists*
I don't mean those placard-carrying mystics proclaiming the end of everything. I had to use "alarmists" because spell-check wouldn't let me get by with the word "alarmers" without flagging it with that squiggly red line. Anyway, these alarmists are those jackasses who pull fire alarms and make anonymous bomb threats or false emergency calls, etc. They get their jollies by causing anxiety. They are timewasters. If caught, they should be forced to watch endless hours of reality television until they scream for their own lobotomies or be made to listen to continuous microphone feedback of a cat coughing up a fur ball (Note to the CIA: I am readily available for hire as a consultant in matters such as these.)

Pet Peeve #10: *Vandals*

Get a job, buy some good stuff, and see how you feel when someone messes with it. I don't know who is worse; the hooligans that paint stupid shit on public things or those who desecrate cemetery headstones...no...I think I'm leaning more toward the monument smashers for their disturbance of eternal peace.

Bonus Peeve: *Adult Toys—No, not that kind! This is a family...never mind.*

There is something a friend of mine accurately described as yet another omen of the impending apocalypse—*adult coloring books*! Seriously? I'm calling bullshit on this and all those cutesy fads and gimmicks. And don't give me that whole therapeutic rationale. Go paint a fucking room in your house like a grownup. Sheesh! What's next, Fun with Chalk? I'm warning you guys; you're getting perilously close to musical chairs group therapy.

Now on to bigger things.

What's in a Name?

Epistle to the Pharmaceuticals

So, if I was in charge of naming things, my first official act of office would be to change the incomprehensible spellings and pronunciations of prescription drugs which make them damn near impossible to remember. I'm sure this is the case for most of us, unless you possess a degree in medicine, pharmacology, or ancient languages, then the Greek and Latin lexical connotations might actually bear some significance for you.

Even when the pharmaceutical companies attempt to shorten the unpronounceable surnames of their chemicals, one would think they would choose names that are simple to say and remember, instead of ones that twist your tongue into a knot. Perhaps they should follow the lead of their illegal drug brethren who use names like horse, big O, snow, and ice, thereby eliminating any confusion in what you are buying.

Lest you think I exaggerate; here's a little quiz to see if you can identify the actual prescription drug from an Aztec language name:

1. Quetzal or Quetenza
2. Coaxoch or Cosentyx
3. Tlaloc or Tnkase

For those of you obsessed with keeping score in such matters, the prescription drug appears second in each pair. See what I mean?

I believe the drug companies should reconsider renaming the nomenclature of their medications, making them simpler and easy for the tongue to negotiate. Instead of drugs whose names just beg for a vowel to interrupt a string of consonants hailing from the latter end of the alphabet, let's assign names which are a snap to pronounce and remember. For example, let's name prescriptions after, say, the Seven Dwarfs of Disney fame. You would have Sleepy, Doc, Grumpy, Sneezy, Bashful, Happy, and Dopey. Not only would these be easy to recall, and most certainly fun to say, but come with the added benefit of actually describing an effect they might have on you.

Look, all I'm saying to you pharmaceutical companies out there is there's no reason not to make this simple for the majority of your customers, who already suffer your unscrupulous and exorbitant prices on chemicals produced for pennies on the dollar. In fact, I think I'll complain about that aspect a little later on.

Now, heigh-ho, heigh-ho, it's off to work I go.

Misery Loves Company

Epistle to the Sloths

Sadly, this pet peeve occurs more frequently than sunsets. You're driving along without a hitch, when up ahead, you catch sight of a car sitting at the stop sign on a side street. A glance in your rearview mirror shows the road behind you to be clear all the way to the nearest coast. Initially, the logical portion of your brain thinks that there is no way, nor any reason for this guy to pull out in front of you. Then, the life experience part of your noodle, screams, "Yeah, but that's exactly what the bastard's going to do," and is validated when the car pulls out just moments before you get there, forcing you to hit the brakes to allow the blockhead in.

Now, you might expect that someone who just committed such a foolhardy act, risking life and limb, must have some kind of emergency. If not, then he surely would have waited the two more seconds for your car to pass, thus giving him safe passage to pull out into the open landscape behind you. But, alas, that never seems to be the case in these situations. This car, that just had to break your motoring roll, proceeds to crawl along at tortoise speed, having apparently exhausted all available energy resources when abruptly pulling out in front of you.

Cursing, you follow behind on that hilly, narrow road, which affords nary an opening to pass the slowpoke and contains enough blind curves to discourage even considering such a maneuver. Meanwhile, cars from two time zones away have begun to line up behind you in what was once an open road, but now has been transformed into an unexpected motorcade.

As the funeral procession continues, tempers and frustrations mount. Suddenly, a car from behind breaks formation and seizes a brief window of opportunity to roar past several other vehicles, as well as your own, slowing down only to flip the bird at the slug in the first car. However, in doing so, he fails to notice the oncoming Ford 150. As both vehicles whirl off to the side of the road in a fiery death-spin, the remainder of the laborious wagon train chugs on, by now filled with a fear that squelches any remaining anger and further rashness.

The convoy continues on its interminable journey—now officially qualifying for parade status—until the perpetrator of all this misery, at last, turns off the road. No one dares to follow, even if it was their turnoff as well, content and delighted to be out from behind the sluggard.

As relief abounds, both speed and spirits pick up once again. That is until up ahead, where at the next right, sits a lone car.

You Don't Say

Epistle to the Babble

I wish someone high up on the media corporation food chain would pull the plug on postgame interviews of athletes and coaches. I mean, what's the point? It's all been said thousands of times before and has become meaningless drivel intended to stretch out advertising time. Following are just a few examples of the statements we have come to expect and fear from postgame interviews:

We gave it our all out there.
We're just taking it one game at a time.
They're a tough team, but our guys managed to put it all together and pull this one out.
I was seeing the ball well tonight.
We got lucky and caught (him, them) on an off night.
It was a (group, team) effort.
Our (offense, defense) picked us up tonight.
I just thank the Lord for giving me the ability to do what I do.
Our backs were against the wall, and our guys came through.
It feels great, but we need to go out there and do it all over again tomorrow.
Thank goodness, we were able to turn it around in time.
It's a great win, but we won't celebrate until we have that championship trophy in hand.

There are games when you just can't catch a break.
His (curve, slider, changeup) kept us off-balance all night.
It feels great to be able to win this in front of these great fans.

And so on, and so on.
Enough said.

Undercover Activity

Epistle to the Anarchists

Hopefully, it's safe to assume that no one will object to my complaining about terrorists. So here goes.

I will begin by saying that even though I am about to poke fun at terrorists—and probably draw a jihad in my direction—in reality, they are no laughing matter. So first, I have a few choice words for you bad guys. I want you to know for certain that if you feel the urge to shoot up a school, movie theater, or church prayer meeting, then there is something incredibly wrong with your wiring, and you should rush to seek immediate help because it's not all about you, assholes. If you're unhappy with your miserable existence, either talk it out with somebody from the sane side of the reality tracks, or go off quietly into a corner and do what you need to do without taking the blameless with you. And as for you religious terrorists; don't go preaching that what you do is ordained by a higher power or some religious dogma, and then go out and slaughter innocents, because no legitimate omnipotence or sacred doctrine would ever condone such acts of barbarism. Hiding your own moral deficiencies within the guise of religion merely constitutes an act of cowardice and ignorance, and is ultimately doomed to produce the opposite effect you had hoped to achieve. Your actions are the acts of ignoble and ignorant individuals.

With that out of the way, I'm now going to tie that in with a subject that is near and dear to all of us, and I do mean very near to us—underwear. I'm not referring to boxers, briefs, thongs, or granny panties; although I suppose they could all qualify if constructed in the right way. No, what I am alluding to is the explosive variety—not explosive, as in Victoria's Secret wow, but explosive as in things that go kablooey!

I'm not sure which represents the better indicator of al-Qaeda's current weakness; the elimination of Osama bin Laden or the fact that they now have been reduced to using underpants to conceal and transport explosives. It wasn't that long ago when terrorists would fill VW vans with explosives and drive into a compound, market square, or building. Now they have sunk so low, as to using jockey shorts with exceedingly elastic waistbands. For obvious reasons, this stunt just doesn't seem to convey the same terrifying effect. Seriously, how much bang can there be in a pair of Fruit of the Boom briefs?

Granted, perhaps while flying at an altitude of 30,000 feet and in close quarters, I can visualize it having more of a scary impact. Nevertheless, I ask again; technically speaking, how much whump can be packed into a pair of tighty-whities? Would it be enough to pop open an overhead bin or rebound a seat into its upright position? To date, the only example of it being attempted on a flight merely caused a crotch to catch on fire. "Pardon me, sir, is that your smoke or are you just happy to see me?"

I realize it's a martyr thing going on and all. Yet somehow, going out with fifty pounds of C4 strapped to your body or in a bomb-laden Renault has just got to create more of a desired result than a pair of chestnuts roasting on an open fire.

Obviously, this subject should be taken more seriously, but when the New York City media reported, in actual fact that then police commissioner, Ray Kelly, complained that he was not *briefed* quickly enough by the CIA with specifics about the al-Qaeda, double agent, underwear plot, you just have to laugh.

After the terrorists attempted the bomb-in-the-shoes strategy, everyone then had to unshod at airport security, making times and lines longer. Now, after this underpants fiasco, just imagine if they deem it necessary for us to disrobe and remove our undergarments. Not only will that further increase the logjam, but also things are going to get pretty ugly, pretty fast.

I venture that most of us were raised hearing that dire, motherly warning of never traveling with holes in your underwear or else suffer unholy humiliation, if God forbid, we were in an accident. Nowadays, if holes are discovered in your skivvies, they might be interpreted by the TSA as evidence of an accidental chemical spillage of an explosive material. In which case, you have a lot of 'splainin' to do. When you think about it, maybe the real terrorist act in these cases is the personal inconvenience, and the discomfiture of stripping, prodding, groping, and scanning in public.

Consequently, I have to ask, where do we go from here, terrorists? Will it be *Sky Mall* magazine with explosive ink, contact lenses as detonator caps, or perhaps dental floss plastique? All I know is, if the worst-case scenarios come true, I for one will not be taking off my nether garment at airport security. Hopefully, they will offer us a choice. If you choose not to take off the undies, then you will be subject to a wedgie of intense proportions to dislodge or disable any contraband material. If this is the case, I will endure the latter option, seeing how it will probably help me to better fit into those diminutive airplane seats.

And a Few to End With

There are so many other pet peeves, too numerous to catalog in this short section. However, in attempting to create an all-inclusive list, I run the risk of offending any that I may have omitted. Still, with that being said, I am now going to list a few more that deserve at least a brief mention.

- Discourteous dolts who yak in theaters during the movie. Look around, motor mouths. Does this look anything like your living room? At ten dollars a pop, you can be sure I want to hear every word, moan, giggle, whinny, and sound effect I paid for.

- Snowplow drivers who seem to fiendishly wait until you've cleared that last shovel of snow from the end of your driveway, before driving down the street and filling it up again. I'm sure there is a special place in hell reserved for you guys.

- Sporting venues that jack up prices on refreshments, which together with astronomical ticket charges, nearly guarantees that college will be delayed for the kiddies. Twelve dollars for a beer? It better be brewed and aged by some Rothschild baron. Isn't it bad enough that tickets cost more than organ transplants?

- Any waitstaff or salesperson who responds to each and every request with, "No problem."

- Commercial parking lot engineers, whose evil designs keep us driving through a maze of turns and berms; intended so we have pass by each merchant in order to exit, or worse, end up in a Bermuda Triangle for lost cars.

- Any Windows operating system—with the possible exception of XP, which must have been designed by a former Apple guy.

- Telemarketers and robo calls that blatantly ignore the No Call Registry.

- People who insist on buying cars with "aerodynamic" spoilers on the back, and then drive as if they're leading a funeral procession.

- The aggrandizement of the never-ending media awards shows, which only serve to stroke delicate egos, provide free publicity, and line the pockets of the networks. We really need to hear the "Get-Off-the-Stage" music on these babies.

- Those people with little or no talent who grab money and fame from the reality show business, and whose programs are as far from being real as Donald Trump.

- Beer and ales that have either a fruity taste or fruit hanging off its glass. That's what sangria is for, people.

- Any banners, maps, or flashing ticker tape news and weather stories scrolling across the bottom of the television screen. No wonder ADD is rampant in the civilized world.

- While I'm there, those intruding ads for the network's own shows that suddenly burst onto the bottom of the screen. They are more distracting and confusing than informative.

- People who have to be first in line for everything; even a funeral. What the hell is your rush?

- Any religion that professes "holy wars."

- Vladimir Putin. Seriously, who does this guy think he's fooling?

- Dental offices that are run like shady car dealerships or auto repair shops, hyping problems that do not exist just to extract our money.

- The restaurant hosts or hostesses who seat you next to a table of squawking kids when there are more empty tables in the establishment than patrons.

- And while I'm at it, the parents who think it's 'okay' to experiment taking their untrained children for "You're-Not-at-Home" situations, such as eating establishments where most people go for a relaxing, quiet repast. It's not the kids' fault, you big dummies, and it's not 'okay.'

- Movie subtitles written in white on light backgrounds that are impossible to read before they disappear.

- Movie subtitles written so small…see above.

- Waitstaff asking if you need more time with the menu and then do not return until the next day and with a new specials sheet in hand.

- The idea that my phone call may be monitored for training or security purposes.

- Spoiled, obnoxious celebrities, athletes and politicians.

- Rally caps

- Helicopter parents

- Excessively loud motorcycles or car radios.

- Zombie apocalypse and vampire shit. Yeah, werewolves, too, come to think of it.

- Any pitching decision made by Joe Girardi.

The Complaints

"What do sad complaints avail if the offense is not cut down by punishment?"

- Horace

While a pet peeve tends to nag at us when it occurs, the grating residue of a complaint remains with us long after the initial trespass.

You Are No Longer Free
to Move about the Cabin

Epistle to the Sufferers

With today's air travel, the only thing that seems to be getting larger is the line at the security checkpoints. Everything else is getting either shorter, smaller, or narrower, including tempers, patience and courtesy.

People who fly first or business class need not bother with this epistle. Little in here applies to you. Still, I'm betting that even some of your flight amenities and services have been tweaked downward as well. Perhaps, it's just a slightly lower thread count on the pillowcase, or your bourbon is aged a few years less. If so, then feel free to stick around.

Predictably, for the rest of us seated behind the curtain, flight amenities have all but disappeared. Even if we were lucky enough to qualify for an in-flight snack, it would most likely consist of a non-alcoholic drink drizzled over ice in a plastic cup and a packet of pretzels, peanuts, or cookies that look like they could be the runts of a vending machine litter. These you can either economically nibble on to provide sustenance until reaching your destination or use them to barter with your fellow passengers for more under-seat space or legroom.

Certainly, there is always the option of buying back some of your depreciated amenities by using the airline's quick-loan approval financing program. Unfortunately, these are usually limited to a threadbare blanket, a marshmallow-sized pillow, and a pair of cheesy earbuds.

Then there's the matter of luggage, which has been subjected to the same downsizing policies. Already restricted in size and number, now if a bag exceeds the poundage limit, you must either pay a surcharge or remove enough clothing items to make the specified weight. At which point you are left to either cram the excess clothing into your carry-on or put them on over your existing clothing and hope for the best at the security pat down and x-ray.

In what can only be described as the Reverse Tardus Effect (with apologies to Dr. Who), the airplanes themselves appear to be bigger on the outside, but the space inside the cabin is most certainly shrinking faster than customer satisfaction.

At 6'3" tall, these increasingly cramped quarters have become even more of a challenge for me personally. It starts with the diminishing width of the aisle between the seats. This went from being reasonably ample to barely waist-sized in breadth—which, according to the airlines, is apparently the size of a post-hunger strike Mahatma Gandhi. This being the case, many of our weight-challenged citizens must now laboriously sidle their way down the aisle to their assigned seating. The end result being endless bottlenecks, while passengers try to locate their seats, find room to store their carry-ons, or grease up their hips to squeeze through a passageway the width of a capillary. And for those already seated, this means a brutal boarding time of tummy thrusts or fanny presses, depending on which side of the aisle you're on.

Overhead storage bins, now reduced to glove compartment dimensions, are crammed with larger carry-on baggage, which previously would have been checked luggage before the restriction limits and fees went into effect. Many of these bags were made larger still, by the extra clothing jammed in from overweight checked suitcases. The stuffed overhead bins, which now resemble the interior of a teenager's closet, are so small and crammed that it is not unusual to find seat 1A's paraphernalia stored in your 14 AB bin, thereby forcing you to find distant accommodations for your own coat and carry-on. Unfortunately, this usually means that the only hope of successfully retrieving your stuff upon landing is that your objects may have shifted during the flight, bringing them safely home to their rightful bin.

Squeezing down the aisle, I am forced to slalom and dodge open bin doors. This is made even more difficult, with the need to bend my tall frame in order to avoid becoming lodged in place and creating yet another aisle gridlock, while awaiting some kind passenger from behind to pass forward his jar of Vaseline.

With each new plane model, the size of the seating area continues to shrink. Carefully shoehorning my body into the coffin-sized space, I now find my knees pressed firmly against the seat in front of me, the armrests snuggly caressing my love handles, and my head rising far above the seat's head cushion, so as to make any snoozing impossible, even if I were so inclined. When the stewardess makes her pre-flight rounds to check on seatbelts and upright seats and trays, she doesn't give me a second glance, as she plainly observes that I am— for all intents and purposes— wedged in place for the entire flight, not to be dislodged even if the plane were to tragically crash and break apart. Heaven forbid, if I ever needed to use the bathroom, it would require the assistance of two beefy flight attendants equipped with the Jaws of Life to extract me from that seat.

Being in such a vulnerable position, things can take a nasty turn for the worse, if the passenger sitting in front of me abruptly decides to be an ass and recline his seat. Instantaneously, my knees are driven towards the back of my seat, violently ejecting my tightly wedged body free and into the overhead compartment. I would now be free to walk the cabin area, if not for the fact that my knees have been relocated to the back of my legs.

As with every other creature comfort aboard the plane, the space under the seat is smaller as well. This can turn out to be a cause of tension between passengers, as the diminished area now becomes a realm of disputed territory. Does this region—which has shrunk to a size unable to accommodate anything larger than a toiletry bag—belong to the passenger paying for the seat above it, or to the passenger behind, who might need the foot/leg room to store a carry-on that couldn't find a home in the congested overheads? Regrettably, thus far, the right of eminent domain remains in question.

Moreover, while I didn't think it was even possible to make airplane bathrooms any smaller than they already were, somehow the airlines accomplished this task as well—probably using some engineering science involving nanotechnology. Nowadays, you don't so much as go *into* one of these bathrooms, as you do *put them on.* This being the case, it is critical always to enter the bathroom in the direction you intend on doing your business, because turning around in this cocoon is not an option. The one upside to this bathroom intimacy is that everything you need is within easy reach, or more precisely, already in contact with your body.

Making this entire flying experience even worse for me is the fact that I suffer from claustrophobia. Because of this, I always try to secure an aisle seat, which at least gives me the semblance of more room, along with a possible escape route. Not being hemmed in on at least one side, mitigates my fear of not being able to get out of the tight place I am in, if I needed to do so in the event of an anxiety attack. Additionally, the outside seat allows me to hang one knee out into the aisle, at least until someone needs to thread the eye of that needle to use the restroom. Yet, the presence of any bodily protuberance into this narrow no man's land is not without its risk, particularly from the bone-crushing assault of the beverage cart as it scrapes its way down the alley between the seats. Once able to navigate this strip of a passage freely, it now grinds and rattles its way down like a mine tram through a shaft.

Another thing that helps me cope with my claustrophobia is to have air blowing on me. This means I need a dependable, working air vent above. In fact, turning it on is the first thing I do upon taking my seat. Of course, I'm sure it won't be long before this too, will be deemed an upgrade. The problem with these vents is that the airflow is usually at its weakest when I need it the most, which is just before the plane takes off and after it lands. During these times, everyone is standing or still lodged in the aisle, making the limited open space even smaller and consequently increasing my phobia. This also happens to be when the air conditioning and airflow in the cabin drops to their lowest levels, causing heat and stuffiness to build, further escalating my sense of dread and anxiety. At this point, if self-calming techniques have not worked, I begin scanning the human barrier beside me for the weakest links on which to unleash my panic attack.

Disembarking the plane, already a nightmare in and of itself, has become even more so with a logjam worse than the one during boarding. Even before the airplane completes its taxiing to the terminal—and in direct disobedience to the pilot's explicit instructions to remain seated until the plane comes to a full stop—bodies immediately begin flooding that crawl space of an aisle and commence to attack the overhead bins in what essentially resembles a feeding frenzy. Of course, the heat inside the fuselage now increases exponentially as the air conditioning and air vent outputs are cut back to minimum survival levels.

Meanwhile, in the aisle, the accumulated mass of warm, squirming early risers attempt to position themselves for departure in the classic "hurry up-and-wait" formation. What this imprudent stratagem has accomplished, however, is to reduce the amount of open space around me, closing me in, and effectively eliminating my escape route for what has now become full-blown claustrophobia. This virtually ensures that a panic attack will need to be dealt with, before I begin clawing my way over Vaseline-coated bodies.

While all this is transpiring, the crew at the front of the plane gleefully captures pictures on their phones of the hilarious spectacle before them. Scenes of passengers jammed in the aisle like a clog in a drainpipe, carry-ons tumbling out of opened bins and onto the heads of the poor suckers still trapped in their seats, and one shot, in particular, of that screaming maniac back at 14A.

This Space: *Not for Sale*

Epistle to the Hustlers

The proliferation of advertising has reached staggering proportions in this country. It's to the point, that if there is an empty space anywhere people have to cast their eyes, then it is considered prime real estate for some corporate plug. The virtual and real landscapes have become so inundated with commercials that they are blocking the things we truly want to see.

The print media has long been the bastion of advertising. Magazines that once featured articles and stories, now intersperse these between several pages of ads on beauty products and ones which encourage you to "talk to you doctor before using." By the time you've flipped through your fourth "continue on to page…" you've completely lost the gist of the article you had been reading. Then, to add insult to injury, when all the pages of the magazine are filled, publishers will insert postcard-sized ads between the pages, which annoyingly fall out upon handling the issue, forcing you to notice them as you pick them up.

Newspapers, no longer content in housing their advertisements within the borders of their newsprint, now stuff their tabloids with circulars, while wrapping the front sections of the paper in additional folded advertisements. Sometimes, just for good measure, the publishers will slap a sticker-ad on the front page to further obscure headlines and stories.

While television has always thrown commercials at us, today, they now seem to be coming from every angle of our flat screens and all in high-definition. Stations have even reached the point of running advertisements about themselves and their lineup of shows, and not only in the normal commercial break spots. Now, they plaster their station logos in the lower right corner of the screen, while occasionally squirting distracting promos for future shows across the bottom of the set in the middle of the show you are trying to watch.

Additionally, both the television and movie industries have shown themselves as the revenue whores they are, by imbedding into their media, product placements for cars, refreshments, technology gear, etc., every chance they get.

Speaking of the silver screen, commercial television is one thing, but when we pay a king's ransom to attend a movie presentation and are then subjected to a barrage of commercials prior to the seemingly endless previews, it is not only wrong, but also downright insulting. Just as infuriating are advertisements on the movie DVDs you have purchased. If Hollywood is going to include commercials at the theaters and in our homes, then the movies should be free. They can take their cut from the exorbitant prices paid at the snack bars if need be.

With the exception of a few static advertisements on fences, sporting events used to be safe havens from rampant commercialism. However, today, it's even hard to concentrate on the game itself with all the flashing ads and video clips on display in full Jumbo Vision. Rotating billboards flip several times an inning or quarter while featuring as many sponsors as possible. *This inning is brought to you by Cranston Foods, featuring the delicious new toaster snack—pasta pockets!* Every segment of the game is broken down into subsidized chunks of time. Of course, the granddaddy of all-things commercial is the Super Bowl, where the rights to the pre-game show, coin toss, kickoff, halftime presentation, and wardrobe malfunctions are sold to and named for some company promoter.

Venues that once sported cherished names like the Polo Grounds, Ebbets Field, the Hoosier Dome, and Candlestick Park are now sold to the highest corporate bidders, who have changed those classic names to such awe-uninspiring ones like the KFC Yum! Center, O.co Coliseum, Qualcomm Stadium, and Minute Maid Park—incredibly once called Enron Field!

Today's teams and players all wear comped outfits and footwear bearing the logos and names of their benefactors. By far, the worse of these sellouts has to be NASCAR, whose drivers and vehicles come festooned in decals and patches covering every open space of fabric or fiberglass.

Go ahead and try to find an open space of some size in your internet browser's window. They are gobbled up by ads that popup, float, flash, and creepier still, follow you down the screen while scrolling.

Parading down the red carpet in donated gowns and jewelry, radiant media stars willingly share the names of the designers of their glitzy attire.

It is hard to imagine this propagation of advertising getting any worse, but with the creativity of the Madison Avenue hawkers, combined with the unbridled avarice of corporations, no vacant space or event is safe. It wouldn't take much of a stretch to envision the iconic Popemobile decked out with an ad—ala NASCAR—for Windex or Bubble Wrap.

Although, not that they haven't tried so far, many companies may soon attempt to attach their branding to the holidays themselves. We may one day hear of Easter by Cadbury, Valentine's Day by Whitman's Sampler, and both of these celebrations and all the rest brought to you by Hallmark.

Soon, we'll have space explorations being presented by Amazon, and search and rescue missions sponsored by Google.

On a positive note, in order to put a dent in our national debt, perhaps we can creatively sell advertising spots for the quagmire that is Congress: *This current Congressional gridlock will be presented to you by Ex-Lax—when movement is difficult,* or *The following filibuster will be brought to you by Dyson vacuums—putting hot air to good use.*

Sadly, the next victim on the ad men's hit list could be nature itself—lots of open space to tap into here. In the near future, we could be seeing signs such as: *This panorama is presented to you by Apple's iCloud Bank—Trust Us, Your Money's Up There Somewhere.* Another could be, *The scenic overlook ahead is brought to you by Dr. Larry's Lasik Lab—It's Looking Good, Because You Are, Thanks to Dr. Larry,* or *This vista is being sponsored by Kodak—Go Ahead and Snap Away. This is a moment!*

It appears that everyone and everything is selling out, but listen up corporate world. You're not getting this guy! I promise not to sell any advertising space on my home, property, or anywhere on my body, so when I look into that mirror in the morning, I just see me—plain and simple.

The preceding complaint was brought to you in part by Hart Awareness Wristbands—Remember to "Wear your Hart under your sleeve."

With Apologies to Hervé Villechaize

Epistle to the Branded

Look. I don't care if you etch the Mona Lisa on your body. My criticism of tattoos is based on my not understanding the attraction of doing bodily harm to one's self in order to preserve in perpetuity, a snake writhing out of the eye socket of a skull. I will admit to tattoos being interesting at first glance, but that's where it ends. I would think having to look at the same picture day after day would soon lose its appeal. At which point, that one of Katniss Everdeen on your forearm—unlike an ugly piece of clothing—can't simply be removed.

Let's be honest. Tattoos do not work for everybody, and yet a lot of people are getting them. Personally, I believe the last individual to pull off the tattoo thing successfully was that notable man of cartoons who ate spinach right out of the can and sported forearms resembling pythons digesting two piglets. Though I, myself, wouldn't get one, I have no issue with tattoos which are concealed from plain sight. It is clear these were acquired for the personal enjoyment of those people or their intimate friends.

The exhibitionists are the ones that bother me. These breathing billboards choose to advertise their tats out in the open in places where clothing seldom ventures. To these people, I have to ask, why? Help me understand. Are you making a statement, a philosophical confirmation, or merely a maudlin expression of emotional endearment? If so, why make it so irrevocable? Why not just get a bumper sticker for your car, start a blog, or send a sappy greeting card? Because sooner or later, loves and viewpoints change, and when they do, you're not only stuck with old beliefs and memorials ingrained in your hide, but now find yourself explaining to others how they are no longer germane to your present life situation.

Perhaps you get this artwork for the straightforward purpose of adornment or accessorizing. Then again, jewelry can accomplish the same thing, and with less permanence. Maybe it's the cool factor, or the need to be conspicuous. However, with so many others doing the same thing, doesn't that dilute your intention? Or is it meant to represent an emblem of accomplishment? *Look at me. I survived an insanely fast needle, which jackhammered ink into my skin, just so I could present this artwork for your viewing pleasure.*

There are those who plaster themselves with, not just a word or simple phrase, but whole passages or paragraphs of text. Please tell me who, besides an awkward stranger, is going to read all that shit? Get a damn T-shirt with some snarky message on it. Then, at least, you will be able to change up your desideratum every once in a while.

As baffling as all this is, I find it nearly incomprehensible that someone would slap a tat on the face. What, pray tell, was your thought process in arriving at that decision? Don't you recall how ticked off you were after that drunken bender, when you awoke to find your "friends" had adorned your face with magic marker? Remember how pissed you were? Well, guess what? That new road map decorating your mug is there to stay, and even more incredible, you were fully cognizant during its creation. You should just try blending into a crowd now with those stigmata of yours screaming, "Here I am (FBI, CIA, state troopers, old girlfriends!)"

Lastly, there are the Walking Canvases. Those people fill every available space of epidermal real estate with one design or another. Their bodies remind me of those internet pages that are so busy with ads, promos, and other superfluous junk that you cannot see the forest for the trees. I would think one or two small, discreetly placed tattoos would be far more effective than having the ceiling of the Sistine Chapel imprinted upon your flesh.

Of course, the big question that remains is what happens to these tattoos when the aging process causes the skin to lose its tautness. I'm thinking those images of faces will begin to resemble our old buddy, Popeye the Sailorman, and all the others will look like they belong in a Salvador Dali painting.

Why not just get a temporary tattoo, which can be scrubbed off? You could try it on for size, and then when you tire of it or Kelly dumps you, have a falling out with MOM, or lose affection for bees, butterflies, mermaids or apocalyptic scenes, then you can wash it off. After you discover that those Chinese characters or Gaelic runes inscribed on your body really stand for *Legless Toad* or *I sure could use some chutney about now*, you can easily remove them. However, getting rid of those ink beauties, which now stain your body tissue, is going to require undergoing a long, painful process, in which you will pay through your nose ring to have done.

Look, I know it's me, but I just don't see the appeal of this fashion trend, especially after considering the pain, the commitment of permanence, and the effect aging will have on those tattoos. I often wonder what this current generation will look like when they become senior citizens. I try to envision what will be going through the mind of young Emma, an assisted-living nurse's aide, as she spoon feeds tapioca pudding to Mrs. Peterson, as her *Don't Tread on Me* tattoo lies in wrinkles along her withered forearm?

A Loss of Innocence

Epistle to the Successors

"There's a lot of ugly things in this world, son. I wish I could keep 'em all away from you. That's never possible." – Atticus Finch in *To Kill a Mockingbird*

What do we say to the kids?

Growing up as a child in the 50's and early 60's, things were simple and straightforward in their nature—at least from a kid's point of view. For the most part, we were carefree and wholesome without even realizing it; taking pleasure from seemingly trivial occurrences. We looked forward to going to the movies, fairs, or athletic competitions. While we might not have admittedly looked forward to school, we felt safe there. Here, the most unnerving thing outside of lost teeth or nosebleeds were the duck and cover bomb drills, during which we nervously giggled because it looked so funny, seeing how none of us had ever seen or heard a real bomb explode before, never mind one of the atomic sort. Sure, we saw some go off on television shows and even witnessed some bloodless shootings on our western, war, and detective shows, but those deaths were always honorable or deserved.

Then, in the mid-60's our way of life began a transformation with the senseless assassinations of our heroes and the divisiveness of the Vietnam War. A Pandora's Box was opened and ideals and ethics morphed into things complicated and confusing, and that was just for the adults. So what must the children have thought?

Although movies, malls, road races, and, yes, even school still provided pleasure for kids, they now took on different perspectives. Before, the main concern in these settings was getting lost or forgetting homework. Nowadays, these places no longer feel so insouciant or invulnerable.

Today's children are now forced to see things through grownup eyes, where even we as adults, are hard pressed to explain the heartbreaking inconsistencies that continuously interrupt the sane and secure world we try to provide for them. In addition, the bloody deaths they now witness on the news and television shows are neither honorable nor justified.

So, what do we say to them on their loss of innocence? Perhaps we should just be honest and say:

Kids, we're sorry. We've accidentally created, for the most part, a world unlike any known before. It is still a beautiful and wondrous place, but now it is a little more unsecured and unpredictable. Over the years, we got smarter, came up with astonishing new ideas, and made some awesome things, but we were not smart enough to envision that in the process, some of them would go terribly wrong and some unsafe things would come to light. If we could go back in time, we would try to do things a little differently, but Mommy and Daddy can't make it better now. Instead, we will try our best to keep you protected from the worrisome things we made. Just know that for the most part you will be safe, so have fun. But always keep aware and alert because you know that we can't always be there to watch over you. It was our job to keep you safe and give you a childhood of carefree innocence, where your only concerns would be poison ivy and bumps in the night. We should have known better, but we didn't. We're sorry.

Car Sickness

Epistle to the Title Holders

One of the worst feelings you can experience is when something goes wrong with your car. Most likely, because we tend to rely so much on its convenience in everyday matters…that, and the fact that whatever is wrong will not be cheap to remedy. This piece first appeared on HumorPress.com, but under a different name to protect the innocent.

Cars…can't live with them, can't blow them up in a public display of anger and frustration.

Let's face it. We've made ourselves as dependent upon these tin lizzies as we have the telephone, television and the versatile Salad Shooter. Perhaps that last example doesn't carry the weight of importance in your home as it does in ours, but the point being, that the limitations of our freedom as bipeds are directly tied to the automobile.

For most of us, the following scenario is all too familiar. You get a new car or a new used car, and most everything goes well during the honeymoon period. You become best buds with your new set of wheels. Then something minor goes wrong, and just to be on the safe side—because your buddy's been so good to you, and you don't want to mess that up—you take it to the garage for a quick checkup and to preserve the status quo of your wonderful relationship. This test-run also serves in vetting the shop, in case you really need to use it someday for a more serious repair. Anyway, you know what happens next. It's like going to a hospital to visit a friend, relative, or just to browse the well-stocked gift shop. Upon leaving the facility, you are suddenly seized upon by a multitude of maladies and end up out of circulation yourself. This happens, of course, because even though people do get well in hospitals, the reason they're there in the first place is that they are SICK, INFECTED, and CONTAMINATED! They are living, breathing, and sneezing Petri dishes, and those exorcised germs abound, turning into angry displaced nomads in search of a new host.

Well, the same thing happens to your car. Let's say it goes into the shop to have some chiropractic alignment done on its tires. But, while it's sitting in there with all those other sick-bay vehicles, a mechanical virus from one of the other afflicted autos manages to worm its way into your car's cooling or exhaust system, and from that point on, there's little that can be done but await the next ailment to appear. And appear it will, with a frequency that's appalling. This car, which had once been so good to you, now becomes a troublesome burden, and that great sucking sound that is heard is its vacuum pump going to work on your bank account.

Allow me to relate a personal experience as an example. A few years ago, I bought a used 2004 car, the make and model of which shall remain anonymous to prevent undue buyer's consternation. The first few months were relatively trouble-free with only a couple of manufacturer recall visits for seat belt ends, body mounts, and a catalytic converter replacement. It was on the last of such visits when I believe the dreaded e-moola virus invaded my vehicle's internal systems. For what followed, was a six month scourge which included tie rods and alignment, two new tires, outer CV boots, throttle position sensor, cleaning and adjustment of throttle plates, flushing the fuel injectors, front brakes with pads and rotors, and rear shoes and drums. The grand total for this healthcare was a few thousand dollars or the equivalent of a new side-by-side refrigerator, a 40-inch HD television, and a state-of-the-art electric range—all of which were to have replaced our art deco artifacts before this vehicular fiasco. Buddy, oh, my buddy.

On my last trip to the garage, the car had been experiencing a thumping sound whenever it ventured into a slow left-hand turn. My now estranged friend was immediately hooked up to the omnipotent diagnostic computer for an hour to determine the mysterious cause of the noise and to devise the most Rube Goldbergesque solution that would assure the loudest sucking sound possible. The computer eventually spit out something about a CV shaft. Yeah, I know, how appropriate. In the meantime, while on safari through the undercarriage, the cyber mechanics discovered the car possessed a leaky transmission pan, a worn radiator hose, assorted threadbare belts, and when tickled under the front shocks, the radio would suddenly blare on speaking in tongues.

Faced with what was surely to be an estimate just shy of the national GDP of Togo, I told the garage that I would take the pan, hoses, and belts, but to hold off on the CV shaft. I informed them that I would turn at dangerously high speeds to avoid the noise and the cost of that repair. The net result was that for a few hundred dollars, I had everything fixed except the problem I had originally brought the car in for.

Painfully, I made out one of the personalized checks for the repairs, which had been provided to me by the garage on an earlier visit. It included their logo and bank account number to expedite matters. As I handed the service manager my next month's mortgage payment, I cynically inquired if I might qualify for any frequent customer miles or something along those lines. All I got in return was a dry chuckle and a smug reminder that the CV shaft would still need to be replaced. "That part alone," he cautioned, "would cost over five hundred dollars." The unspoken message being that by the time my guys finished tinkering, the five hundred dollars would look like the steal of the deal.

Being utterly frustrated by this time, I carelessly quipped, "Is that the best you can do? Don't you have anything in a gold or platinum, with maybe a laser-interfaced doohickey? Wait... I just remembered. I still have some equity in my lawn mower, so why don't we just go ahead and plate the whole damn shaft with cubic zirconia?" The service manager simply smirked, but with a nuance that said, "Be sarcastic all you want, big boy, but we own you now."

There are times when I think it would have been best for all parties involved, if I had just left my car hooked up to that diagnostic computer to serve as its life support system. That way, I could keep it alive until needy and suitable recipients could be found for the remaining healthy parts of the car. However, based upon the shop medical records, this would include only the intermittent windshield wipers and cup holders.

I would, of course, come to visit my old buddy on occasion, just to maintain the semblance of a relationship. When the cost of the hookup exceeded the cost of the repairs, I would instruct my attorney to have the plug pulled. Then, when the car finally collapsed into its own oil pan, I could donate the remains to a mechanic training school.

Cars…you can't live with them, and you can't push them off a precipitous cliff with a smirking service manager gagged and duct-taped to a state-of-the-art CV shaft.

Parking Lot Drones

Epistle to the Abandoned

They come at you from any direction, and most of the time, you'll never see them coming. Sometimes people operate them, but most times, they act on their own. Yet in the end, it still comes down to being a stupid human blunder. I am referring, of course, to that scourge of commercial parking lots—the unattended shopping cart.

Rather than secure their carts in one of the many surrounding corrals, negligent shoppers, due to laziness, inconsideration or both, simply choose to abandon their carriages, scattering them about the parking lot, placed in prime position to embark upon a course of destruction at the first puff of wind or gravitational tug.

(*I now ask that you please read the following two sentences with as much dripping sarcasm as allowed by MLA standards.*) Maybe these patrons were just far too tired after their laborious shopping safaris to escort their carts the short distance to a designated drop-off area; thereby reducing the risk to other vehicles of sudden impacts from these unrestrained handcarts. Yes, I'm sure that must be the reason, and not my first gut-reaction thoughts about laziness and inconsideration. Because if any of these neglectful ninnies (*You can drop the sarcasm now. I'll take over from here.*) ever came out of the store to find one of these metal missiles snuggled up to their own car, where it had left its dented kiss, then they would surely understand the anger and frustration the rest of us feel in such circumstances. Just that little bit more effort could have prevented this entire miserable event.

On average, shopping carts can weigh in at anywhere from thirty to sixty-five pounds, depending on size and material, but even a plastic one can pick up enough inertia to dent a car door or knock an elderly customer on his or her tushie. So how about putting some rubber bumpers on those carts? They just might prevent some of this damage. I know this will cost more, and perhaps the carts will not nestle into each other as nicely as they do now. Nevertheless, I'm okay with the prices of some merchandise going up to cover this extra cost—think perhaps tofu and broccoli. And it really doesn't bother me if the line of corralled carts is crooked, seeing that my OCD is completely under control now. I also realize that this is just a secondary solution to the actual problem—those lazy no-goodniks who don't do the civil thing by returning their carts. Still, there is as much a chance of reforming them as there is of finding a bagger at checkout who doesn't sadistically overload your bags.

To make matters worse, these neglectful shopping cart people employ a variety of methods in the display of their negligent behavior. Some will attempt to present themselves as "fulfilling their duty" by jacking one end of their shopping cart onto the grass berm at the end of their parking space. But instead of removing this obstacle from harm's way, it only serves to inhibit someone else from using that spot with half the cart sticking down into the space. Additionally, this further jeopardizes other cars. With the cart now perched in an angled position, it is poised to roll down into any car, whose owner is foolish enough to park near it. The most ludicrous thing here is that the amount of effort required in hauling that metal beast onto the median, just had to have been more than a walk to the nearest cart round up.

Then there are other times when these loafers, upon noticing that another abandoned cart has already been stranded in a nearby space, decide to add to it, reasoning in their silly, little way, that one more won't matter. It's not long before there is a whole herd gathered in what is now their own makeshift, borderless corral, setting the stage for a madcap stampede of demolition derby proportions at the first strong gust of wind.

Occasionally, a few scofflaws will take their carts off the property in order to transport their goodies home. At the very least, this removes the immediate danger of collision in the parking lot. Unfortunately, what happens is that most of these carts are discarded after their use. Then, if they were abandoned in their upright positions, and being away from the rest of the herd, they can go rogue, committing the same kind of devastation, but in a different habitat. Other times, these AWOL carts are deserted on their sides to become unauthorized urban sculptures.

While I'm at it, just who was the enterprising person that came up with the idea of grocery carts camouflaged as cars to entertain the kids while cruising the aisles? Not only are these rolling obstructions obnoxiously bulky, taking up a whole parking space by themselves, but they are also responsible for numerous accidents and aisle jams in the stores. With their need to make excessively wide turns, they oftentimes wipe out end display cases, causing further delays in the flow of traffic. This is made even more unpleasant with the car's passengers screaming bloody murder for no good reason at all, fraying customers' nerves and setting off sprinkler systems.

Another irksome mystery has even consumer scientists baffled. This is the phenomenon, which occurs upon first entering the store and grabbing a cart. Nine times out of ten, it will have either a bum wheel that wobbles more than Katherine Hepburn, or it will suddenly stop turning, causing the cart to jerk abruptly to one side. Many times, this bad wheel doesn't commit itself until after your cart is full, when it will unexpectedly stop spinning altogether. Then you're stuck dragging or pushing this metal cage around the store until checkout. Yet, once outside and abandoned, these same carts will miraculously roll true in their kamikaze dive towards your parked car.

Rarely are the bozos that deserted their carts caught. If I had my way, I would like to see more parking lot security, specifically on the prowl for these offenders. Perhaps this staff could be reassigned from their present positions as store greeters or those who change the service order numbers in the deli department. Then those thoughtless parking lot rascals could be ticketed and fined for their irresponsible and offensive actions. The penalties collected could then be applied towards the purchase of rubber bumpers for the carts. If a runaway cart is involved in an accident with another customer's car, then the culprit should be severely punished, along with their offense recorded and sent to all commercial retailers that provide shopping carts. The consequence should also include more than the reprobate filing an insurance claim. That would be letting him off easy and might not necessarily bring home the central point of the lesson here.

I'm thinking these people should also be made to shop without the use of a cart for a specified amount of time. Then they would be forced to carry their merchandise around the store by hand and to their vehicles. Repeat offenders might even be made to serve some time as human bumpers, lashed to the front of the carriages to aid in the prevention of accidents. Then again, I guess that might be putting the horse's ass before the cart.

Beasts of Burden

Epistle to the Guardians

I happen to be one of those humans who are not a big fan of pets. Please understand, it's not that I don't like animals, because I do. I just prefer seeing them from afar like in zoos, pictures, movies, or on television. In fact, growing up, I had my fair share of dogs, fish, turtles, and even a fussy iguana. While the fact remains that, none of these creatures is still around, this is more attributable to species longevity rather than owner incompetence, and yet, it's probably a closer call than makes me feel comfortable.

I recognize that there are multitudes of pet lovers out there who consider their animals to be members of their immediate families. I understand this form of reasoning and am accepting of this cute, though bizarre familial arrangement. To all of you, I say, thank goodness for people like you, since it's not going to be me watching over these critters so they don't end up underfoot—most especially my own. After all, I have a hard enough time making certain I don't walk into an open ditch somewhere. So why on earth would I volunteer my services to taking care of some other creature?

Presently, my goal is to simplify life in as many ways as possible. The kids are raised, colleges and weddings are in the past, the home is paid off, and retirement has settled in around me. This being the case, I do not want nor do I seek any new responsibilities, especially any that require tending to other living things (My wife, of course, being the exception, seeing that she has been grandmothered in, and we have this longstanding, reciprocal, managerial agreement in place.) So, it's simplicity I crave right now. I genuinely don't want any of my daily decisions to be based on whether or not it will affect Ringo, Mr. Janks, or Pretty Boy.

When you own a pet, you also own all the obligations that are leashed to it. This means you will suddenly find yourself tethered to the feeding and bathroom schedules of your furred, scaled, or feathered new family member. Soon, you'll find yourself cutting short social engagements in order to head home and let Duke out to "do his business." And if you're going to be away for longer periods of time, you'll need to make "arrangements" for your pet. Either you will have to find a fellow animal lover to pet-sit, pay a hefty room and board fee at the kennel, or as a last desperate step, take Ginger along with you, and you know how pleasantly problematic that can be.

Then there are the collateral expenses that accompany pet ownership: licenses, shots, enclosures, food, vet visits, and grooming, to name just a few. In the long run, it's probably cheaper to put your kids through college—well, maybe not quite, but at the very least, in return for your generosity, your pet will shower you with unflagging love and loyalty, instead of snarky looks and piles of laundry.

Added to these costs are those of household maintenance to repair damage to furniture and floors, and the cleanup of excretory accidents (Just to be clear. I am now referring to the pets; although, I suppose it could just as easily apply to the other subjects in the preceding paragraph.)

Furthermore, you will need to be very careful that the pet you select is compatible with any existing children in the home and that it can tolerate poking, prodding, tugging, and sudden, loud, unexplainable shrieks at any given moment.

Of course, there will be the need for family photos of your pet as well. This is fine, but please be kind and keep them safely confined to your wallet or phone. Believe me when I tell you that I, personally, do not wish to see them, no matter how cute you or your pet-loving friends think they are. To me, it's like looking at baby pictures. They all look the same, so why bother? Besides, I can barely tolerate those of your kids, so oohing and ahhing over those of another species is just not in my wheelhouse.

Oh, there's one last thing. If I happen to come visit, please, please, do not let your slobbering, groin-sniffing, tail-thumping dog come greet me at the door or at any time during my stay. Also, don't let your shedding, claws-ready-to-anchor-themselves-into-my-skin, cat pounce onto my unsuspecting lap, and then say to me, "Look, Snuggles wants to play, or is just being friendly, or really seems to like you," because, rest assured, there is a feeling of mutual distaste there. It's just something we can sense in one another. So, I beg of you, please lock up your family pet member whenever I come a-calling, for both our sakes. Besides, I'm sure you don't want him or her anywhere near me if I happen to fall into an open ditch or something like that.

The Worst of the Bunch

Epistle to the Defilers

I don't give a whit if anybody calls me a curmudgeon, crank, or old fart about this next complaint of mine. In fact, I'm betting there are a lot of regular folk out there who would back me up on this one. For this affront is an environmental crime and is committed by the lowest of those self-centered bottom feeders—the litterers!

Just where do these people get off shedding their refuse onto public or private property with such reckless abandon. I'm fairly certain it's not one of our God-given, constitutionally approved, inalienable rights of life, liberty, and the pursuit of untidiness. These morons (I'm warning you now that I will be ransacking my thesaurus for synonyms for these reprobates) don't give a second thought—if they ever had a first one—about getting rid of their clutter anywhere or at any time. They do this with impunity and with the egocentric assumption that someone else—whose cortex neurons are actually connected—will pick up after them. Worse, they don't even care if it's picked up at all. As long as it's not messing up their personal space, it's not their concern.

To be clear, I'm not referring to those big-time polluters responsible for heinous oil spills, toxic dumping, air contamination, and bad television programming. Although these immoral corporations poison our water, soil, and air and are criminally and morally reprehensible, they are beyond the scope of this complaint or any contempt I can spew in this short piece. The individual litterer is the person that twists my temper dial to the maximum here. After all, it's on the personal level that we common people can do our part in keeping our living spaces neat and tidy. Those who choose to foul our landscape with their obnoxious leavings do so with intent, proving beyond a doubt that these descendants of one-celled organisms haven't journeyed far along the evolutionary trail, and even then, deposited their litter along the way.

Whether walking or driving, these monads will carelessly toss their garbage on the ground or in the water with absolutely no regard for moral responsibility or the environmental consequences of their odious actions. The world is their junkyard, and everyone else their handmaidens, who get to pick up after these spoiled *shitniks* (When I get angry, as I am now, I don't even bother with the thesaurus and just make up terms, as an expression of frustration and my not being on clear-thinking ground.)

I happen to live on the corner of a fairly busy street on one side and a moderately active one on the other. My lawn and the streets accompanying them are therefore easy targets for the flotsam and jetsam left behind by this parade of defilers as they pass by. Having consumed or used a product, they believe there is no need to keep it in their cars or pockets for subsequent proper disposal. Not when there is a whole wide world out there to remove it from their displeasure. I am continuously clearing bottles, cans, fast food wrappers and cartons from my lawn and the nearby streets. I have even found several unidentifiable metal parts, which I can only hope came from their cars and not from passing airplanes or the International Space Station. That way, there's at least the chance for a little retribution, when their automobile is rendered inoperable somewhere down the road.

These half-wits have dumped whole bags of garbage in the middle of the street, and I've even found a love seat romantically deserted by the side of the road. Late one night, after hearing a loud crash outside by my mailbox, I looked out in time to see a pickup truck squealing away after dropping off one of those old-timey television consoles onto the street. I'm telling you— shitniks!

Go to any sports venue from high school to professional, and after the game, just take stock of the amount of rubbish left behind by the spectators, even though there is an embarrassment of trash bins situated everywhere they would have to walk past or around. If confronted, these nincompoops usually proclaim some defensive position along the lines of, "These places have people to clean up this stuff. We'd be costing them their jobs if we did it for them." To that, I ask…really? Are you seriously that fucking dumb? How much effort does it take on your part to clean up after yourself? It's your mess—you deal with it. Perhaps you thought the cost of your cola included the picking up of the container off the cement floor, where you so casually dropped it. How much inconvenience is it to take care of your own debris? For goodness sakes, teach your children, who are watching you, to do the right thing. Then maybe the maintenance staff, whom you care so much about, might actually have time to fill the soap dispensers, clean your urinals, and empty the trash bins—Oh, wait…that's right. The trash isn't in there, is it, Boopsie?

These miscreants don't even respect National Parks and Memorials. Candy wrappers, cigarette butts, and other assorted detritus lay offensively right next to the plaques, markers, flowers, flags, and statues. They are strewn about on scenic trails, overlooks, and beaches. The real tragedy is that much of their plastic rubbish has a good chance of being around longer than the parks and monuments themselves, serving as a lasting memorial to their idiocy and selfishness.

Addendum

I decided to add this last part, seeing that it is somewhat related to the whole littering issue. For obvious reasons, I do not hold the same measure of rancor towards these offenders as the self-absorbed baboons mentioned above. This is mainly because their litter is not technically trash, and their target areas are specific sites, which consequently limits the negative impact of its dispensation.

I am referring to those people with the inexplicable compulsion to toss their spare coinage into any and all large basins of standing water. If this basin happens to contain anything resembling a fountain, then the unsolicited contributions increase proportionately.

This impulse probably has its origin in the folklore of those old wishing wells, where one paid a price for the granting of one's desire. Over time, as these relics disappeared from the landscape, people began using fountains and pools to satisfy their urge to lob money into water. While at first, these folks may have tossed for wishes with their coins, nowadays it seems most donors just go for the coin toss and ask nothing in return. Even though the history of the old wishing wells might have been forgotten by many, for some unknown reason, water still triggers an innate reflexive action to pitch pennies. The sight of coins dotting the bottom of any pool of water appears to have the same contagious aspect as that of witnessing a yawn.

Nevertheless, I maintain that coins thrown into fountains in this manner, still constitutes polluting at worst, and littering at best. This spectacle has become so widespread that no body of standing water is safe, from fountains—be they public or private, decorative or commemorative—to last winter's large potholes. If it's wet and shallow, it seems to beckon specie like a persistent panhandler.

The Rants

"I'm not ranting. I possess a perspective here that you people, who are locked in the ivory basements of your own sub-cultures, simply do not possess."

- Bruce Sterling

I guess the best way to introduce this last section is simply to say that a rant is a complaint that got a little out of hand. It's usually prompted by what is perceived to be gross misconduct on the part of an individual or a larger entity such as a corporation, a group of people, or wildlife in general. As a result, rants tend to be more developed in their scope, and therefore more protracted in their length and derisiveness. Please be advised.

Weather or Not

Epistle to the Fearmongers
A modified form of this tirade first appeared in The Hartford Courant in 2012.

To start with, let's establish the fact that I live in the Northeast, where local boy, Mark Twain once noted, "If you don't like the weather in New England, just wait a few minutes." If you've ever lived in this neck of the woods, you'd fully appreciate the tongue-in-cheek truth in that observation. We expect it all and we get it all. So why then, has reporting on the elements suddenly taken over our airwaves? When did weather become the main news story each night? And I don't mean those stormy bad boys such as hurricanes, tornados, and blizzards, but rather the ordinary, run-of-the-mill storms and other tropospheric tics we experience each and every day. It now seems every unnamed snowstorm and summer afternoon thunderstorm warrants that regularly scheduled broadcasting be preempted for "special reports." What follows is a half-hour or more of photos and videos of fallen trees, downed power lines, charging snowplows, minor street flooding, and soggy on the scene reporters. Interspersed with these images are colorful maps displaying looped Doppler radar splotches to accentuate the peril that is upon us. *As you can see, Waterbury is being hit with heavy red right now, but that should soon be turning to green, before tapering off to yellow by the rush hour drive home.*

Just when the preemptive storm report is mercifully over, now it is time for the regular news, which leads off with—you guessed it—the interminable storm account. Did we really need to miss Ellen dancing with that adorable tuxedo-clad cockatoo?

I recently returned from a little winter break in Florida, and besides the obvious differences of warmth and no snow, the other very noticeable disparity was the lack of sensationalism with regards to the reporting of weather. Instead of trying to have the weather carry their broadcasts, the local stations actually reported on the news with just a five minute interruption for atmospheric conditions.

Up here, the first snow of the season sets off a flurry of activity in the meteorology departments of local news stations, the intensity of which, I imagine, is only equaled by the feeding frenzy of sharks in nature. After a long, dry summer, (there's only so much hype to be had with the threat of thunderstorms and flooding), those first fluffy flakes signal an unbridled opportunity for weather mania. There is so much more that can be done with ice, wind, snow, sleet, and that hideous hydra-headed phenomenon known simply as a "wintry mix."

Even before that first flake melts from existence, giddy forecasters are revving up the OHNO (Overly-Hyped News Operation) engine, which will render perspective and common sense useless. You can almost hear these animated prognosticators in the newsroom, excitedly debating what to name this first snow event, "I know, let's call it Apocalypse!"

"No, no…Armageddon sounds much more calamitous!"

Beginning in mid-November, these stations start running stories about the winter preparations being done by local communities, from the stockpiling of salt to the tuning up of snowplows. They will use these images and others like them as propaganda to incite a bomb-shelter mentality among their viewers. *Winter is not just coming. It is here, people! So get going! Gather those batteries, blankets, food staples, shovels, roof rakes, and for God's sake, fill those bathtubs with water! Don't you love your family?*

What's happened here? The weather used to be something you mentioned in passing with strangers or in awkward social situations when the conversation lagged.

Now the local news has three regularly scheduled half-hour slots, starting at 5:00 p.m. Each half-hour will give a weather report every ten minutes. The first segment gives the current weather conditions with a hint of the misery to come. The second weather report will repeat the current conditions, but add in the evening and next day forecasts, along with teasers for their third installment of fear and loathing, which will come along in ten minutes. When this report finally airs, everything from the previous two reports will be rehashed along with the dismal predictions for the rest of the week. Then this whole formula will be repeated all over again in each of the two following half-hour news slots. That's a nightly dose of nine weather reports in less than ninety minutes and when commercials are figured in, it leaves very little time for any real news. What's more, if there is a genuine chance for a "significant" Nor'easter to develop, then time will be extended on either end of these broadcasts. And, God help us, if there is a blizzard! The local news will hold regular programming hostage for days on end, while they blather on with the same gloom and doom forecasts.

Nowadays, each local media station employs its own "storm team," which becomes the featured headliner on the commercials for its station. At the first pixel of precipitation on the radar screens, these dedicated troops muster at ungodly hours to brave the driving snow or pelting raindrops in the red Doppler zones. Their droning commentaries repeat themselves like the looped radar smudges on their green screens. If for some reason we didn't hear or believe them, they are further reinforced by warnings, closings, and parking bans, scrolling across the bottom of our television sets ad nauseam. Of course, all of this won't matter a hoot to those people truly affected by the storm, seeing that they lost power two hours ago and will miss out on all this excitement. They may be in the dark, but not being exposed to this frenzied hard sell, just might be the silver lining in their cumulonimbus clouds.

A rational person might ask the reason for all this media buildup. Maybe it's the competition between stations to be first on the air with the latest snippet of news, no matter the measure of importance or threat level involved. Perhaps it's because they are on the air so often, there is a need to fill all that time. Consequently, they sensationalize ordinary weather, casting a fear of calamity on the outside atmosphere and getting everyone's undies in a twister. It's as if they believe the real news of the day could not carry their broadcasts. Certainly, there must have been a stock market event, coup d'etat, or celebrity meltdown somewhere on their Doppler radar.

All this relentless crying of wolf has had an anesthetizing effect on us viewers. How are we to know when a genuine meteorological catastrophe is coming, when every little blip is treated as the End of Days? And if by chance, there truly is a real weather tempest, you can bet it will receive more coverage and air time than a presidential election.

I remember when we New Englanders were described as being of "hardy stock." We were familiar with the seasons and what they brought to the table. Secure in this understanding, we went about our lives with minimal stress about the weather conditions. With hardly a second thought, we knew what to do when Mother Nature spilled her nastiness on us. Today, with this need to grab ratings, media stations have resorted to fear-mongering tactics to keep viewers tuned in to their monotonous montage of video clips and catastrophic warnings. Accordingly, they have taken our hardy New England stock, curled it up into the fetal position and placed it in some far corner of the family storm shelter, amid the water bottles, non-perishable food items, and the wall of flashlights and batteries.

Still, we have no one to blame but ourselves if we fall for this hype. Don't let them fool you into thinking they are providing a public service. They are a business, and the bottom line is money and viewers—mostly money. The more anxiety they can create, the more they hope you will continue to watch, and the more advertising they can sell. So to all the local stations and their meteorological tactical teams, I boldly say, you don't "*Have my back*," or "*Are on my side*," or "*Are in my corner*." Just responsibly report the news and leave me out of it! I know you're under a ton of corporate pressure to use the fear tactics and propaganda, but still, do you have to act so smarmy when reporting this bullshit?

Look…it's a storm. Thunderstorms and winter storms have

been around since we've had an atmosphere. We all know what they are like and what to expect from them. Trust us, we know the drill: stay away from windows during a storm and don't use the phone or shower in a thunderstorm. Don't overexert when shoveling or playing Twister—especially shoveling, and stock up on water, food, shovels, flashlights, batteries, and beer. We know all that, but choose to ignore it anyway. So stop badgering us. It's not like we live in some remote area of Siberia. Most of us live only a stone's throw away from a store window within the city looting limits.

If anyone reading this thinks that, I'm suggesting that these analysts shouldn't be giving us a warning shot across the bow, then that would be a faulty assumption. I'm all for a forecast, but it must be responsibly tempered so as not to generate any needless public duress that will have our fellow citizens locked in bloody death struggles over the last Dasani or Slim Jim down at the corner convenience store.

It's time to bring reason back into the equation, or the next thing we may witness will be a special weather coverage, because today has far too much sunshine. We will need to be instructed on how to handle this phenomenon, or it becomes too mild and perfect and we will have all but forgotten that it is safe to go outdoors on days such as these, because all their air mass hysteria is clouding our judgments.

When I was a kid, each of the television stations had only one weatherman named something like Hank, Butch, or Gabby, and all he had to work with was a wet finger in the wind and a window to the outside. He showed us simple maps with air pressure circles and bumpy weather front lines that he manually moved around like pieces on a chessboard. He didn't waste time with the weather we were having at the moment either, because we all had those magic windows to the outside and knew how to use them. Instead, he gave us his best guess forecast for the weather to come in the next twenty-four hours, because back then, anything beyond that time frame was pure science fiction and a crap shoot at best. It was a quick and concise report—in and out, and now time for sports with Tex. And we didn't mind a smidge if his prediction lacked the early warning, pinpoint accuracy of today's meteorological war rooms, because it at least gave us something to complain about with our neighbors.

At today's stations, each weather team lays claim to having the very latest forecasting equipment, which apparently none of their competitors have in their own arsenals. With these, they scan the skies for any drop, flake, or pellet of precipitation. After all, we need to know as soon as possible that a threat could materialize, so we can make the appropriate preparations. If a storm of any caliber were to strike, emergency broadcasts and notifications will flood the local airways until the last vestige of falling wetness hits the ground. These endless hours will be filled with those same brave weather soldiers, who are placed in harm's way within the teeth of the storm's fury, standing atop a Himalayan pile of plowed snow in whiteout conditions, or on the beach while hurricane winds and storm surge waves buffet them about like scraps of paper. Even though you won't be able to hear a single word they are saying, you admire their dedication as they demonstrate to you the ill effects nature's worst can have on the human body in spite of the obvious contradiction in their warnings that you stay safely inside. Then again, they are the professionals.

Even after weather every ten minutes for ninety minutes, the local stations will still flash their ominous warnings across the bottom of our sets during subsequent television shows: *How much snow is coming? How cold will it get? Are your affairs in order?*

Just what happens if these forecasters are wrong, or at the very least, off the mark with their alarming prophesy? Is there any remorse shown or an apology given for having unnecessarily terrified their viewers? Are you kidding? Without as much as a word of contrition for their irresponsible behavior that stressed out the public, and pitted citizen against citizen in the aisles of grocery and hardware stores, they continue as if they had not incessantly warned us the previous day of the coming of a storm of biblical proportions, not witnessed since the Great Deluge. Oh, maybe they might mention that the storm tracked a little further south, so we didn't get hit with the brunt of its wrath, but did they think to mention this possibility the day before? Absolutely not. That would have ruined their 24/7 coverage of what turned out to be a rather normal weather event. *Hey! No one died from the blowing snow. No one froze to the ground, and no one, thank God, ran out of batteries!* Honestly, not only should these stations be made to publicly apologize, but also since they're already out there, they should be forced to shovel every sidewalk and driveway of this "epic" snowfall.

All I ask of the local news media is to use a little levelheaded perspective when it comes to the weather. Don't overstate it and don't treat us like we're small children, never having experienced falling moisture before. Don't over publicize it. Just hold off until one of your many regularly scheduled news slots before giving us the story. We can wait—honest. Until then, if need be, we can always use our windows to see what's going on—staying a safe distance back, of course. And if it truly is a severe weather situation, just ticker tape a warning across the bottom of the screen, if you can manage to get it around the other ground clutter down there like the station logo, what's on next, and parking bans and cancellations.

So please, no more scaring us about normal weather events, because we have enough to worry about with all these long-term climate change effects going on. Just get in and out with the forecast, and then maybe we can get back in time for the verdict from the preempted Judge Judy case, because if I'm being honest here, that's really what prompted this rant in the first place.

Perhaps Henry Wadsworth Longfellow, a fellow curmudgeon, had the most judicious advice for us, "The best thing you can do when it's raining is to let it rain." Amen to that, brother.

Minimum Rage

Epistle to the Publicans

As retired empty nesters, my wife and I eat out regularly two or three times a week. We simply find it easier that way. No one has to cook or clean up, and we can each order whatever we like. Over the course of time, however, I've noticed that service in these establishments has become less personal and more scripted. Perhaps it's the inevitable fallout caused by the preponderance of big restaurant chains. To give their patrons a more consistent dining experience, restaurant staff are required to recite rote expressions and responsibilities are regimentally divided. Or maybe it's due to the fact the underpaid and overworked waitstaff are thrown into a mosh pit of customer deportment and eccentricities, to which, this formality serves as a buffer.

Whatever the reason, I sometimes find myself attempting to alter the regular routine by interacting with the staff other than just the ordering of food. As a result of this quirk of mine, I often find myself on the business end of a threat from my wife that usually ends with the words "dining alone." It seems my wife views this added participation of mine as both foolish and unnecessary. She may be right about that, but sometimes it simply can't be helped; it being one of my vexing idiosyncrasies.

I offer the following scenario to demonstrate this point better.

Arriving at the restaurant, my soon-to-be former dining partner and I are led to our table by a charming young lady bearing the nametag, *Holly*. Now, even though three-fourths of the tables in the establishment are empty, Miss Holly seats us next to the one with two harried parents and their five-pack of wild creatures posing as children.

Before I could ask Holly if the score of vacant tables were purposely being quarantined to prevent a salmonella outbreak, she hurriedly rattles off that John will be our server and will be over shortly. That being said, she makes a hasty getaway, sensing that the distempered brood seated next to us had begun eyeing her as fair game.

True to Miss Holly's word, our server does arrive in short time. While using a menu to wipe off the detritus which has made its way over to our table from the cast of the Little Rascals, he asks, "How are we this evening?"

Before I can respond with, "Fine, with the exception of the five little headaches next door," he sallies forth into his scripted introduction.

"My name is John, and I will be taking care of you this evening."

"Well, John," I say, "what exactly does that mean? I only ask this because I couldn't help but notice that it was that perky, little teenager named Holly that greeted us upon our arrival and proceeded to seat us next to the Rugrats. If you were taking care of us, I would think we might have procured your services at the meet and greet so that we might have avoided sharing this space with the Katzenjammer Kids."

"I'm sorry, sir. That is the job of the hostess, but if you would prefer another table, I could accommodate you with that."

Before the words, "That would be fine," made it to my lips,

I felt the warm, loving glow of my wife's glare, and quickly changed them to, "No, this will do." However, casting a quick glance at our neighbors, I added, "Besides, I read somewhere that predators are attracted to movement. So we'll stay put."

Satisfied, John continued, "May I start you off with something to drink?"

"Are you serious? Can't you hear the Golden Horde pillaging and ravaging over there? You need to ask if I want something to drink."

At this point, my wife intervened with her request for water with lemon.

"And I'll take bourbon in one of those German steins if you have any."

"Perfect," John says, "I'll get those right to you."

"Oh, and John," I say, "send one of those over to the Dalton Gang with five straws. Maybe it will calm them down a little."

John apparently was not taking me serious, as he chuckled and moved on.

Table conversation between my wife and I proved difficult with all the ambient noise, but I still heard enough to recognize that I was getting the *I-don't-know-why-you-do-that-because-nobody-gets-your-sense-of-humor* speech.

In short time, John returns with our drinks, and I couldn't help but notice that the steins are not the size they used to be.

"Have we decided what we would like?" he asks.

As my wife began ordering her meal, I became engaged in watching the five man junta at the next table stage a coup d'état on their parents in what I could only surmise was an attempt at premature emancipation.

"And for you, sir?"

"I'll have the baked stuffed shrimp, but could I have French fries in place of the wild rice pilaf with mushrooms?"

"I'm sorry, sir. We cannot offer substitutions with the entrees."

"Cannot or won't, John? I'm no head chef, but if we're being honest here, it seems to me to be a simple culinary maneuver of not scooping rice onto the plate and then dumping the contents of the fry basket into the space where the rice would have been. Help me out here, John. I mean, who in your kitchen can't handle such a straightforward task, and should I be worried about the more difficult culinary undertakings?"

"Again, I'm sorry, sir, but the restaurant has a strict 'no substitution' policy."

Exasperated, I say, "I really do not like mushrooms, so I will have the rice pilaf without the mushrooms."

I'm sure equally exasperated, John says, "I'm afraid that is not possible, as the rice already has the mushrooms involved."

"Involved?" Really? "Then just give me rice without mushroom involvement."

"I'm afraid that would also constitute a substitution, sir."

"No, John, technically, that would be more of an omission than a substitution."

John remained adamant. I will give him that.

"Actually, sir, you would be substituting rice pilaf for rice pilaf with mushrooms."

"Now, John," I say, "that doesn't make any sense. If I ordered a steak dinner, but didn't want sour cream on my baked potato, would that be considered a substitution?"

"Well, no, the sour cream would be more of an added topping. In this case, though, the rice already has the mushrooms in it."

Sensing a weakening in John's spirit, I went for it.

"John, please, can't you take care of me like you said you would? Can't I have the fries?"

"I'll see what I can do," he says and hustles away.

I chanced a look at my wife, who had remained a silent, but undoubtedly disappointed witness to this transaction.

"I mean, whatever happened to the old 'no problem' response from the servers?" I asked, most likely rhetorically.

Mercifully, the Green Street hooligans next to us, who were running rampant around their table, overturning condiment containers and lighting them on fire, broke the chilly silence.

Our salads soon arrived, but were served to us by someone other than John.

"I'm sorry," I said, "but John is taking care of us. These must be meant for someone else."

"No, they're yours," the interloper said, "I'm just helping John out."

"I see."

It wasn't long before yet another stranger appeared out of nowhere to fill our pessimistic-looking water glasses, and disappeared just as swiftly.

A short time afterwards, though momentarily distracted by the arcane, ceremonial chanting of the nearby devil spawn, I barely managed a glimpse of another passing waitstaff, who swooped in and collected our finished salad plates without so much as a word being spoken. I didn't say anything to my wife so as not to concern her, but I was beginning to worry that maybe John had not taken kindly to our prior friendly banter, or had his feet put to the fire for agreeing to a forbidden substitution.

So I was noticeably relieved when John finally made a return appearance at our table to tell us that our entrees should be out shortly. He nodded towards my empty bourbon glass, and asked if he could get me another drink.

"No, I'm good, John, thanks. But I must tell you that I'm a little concerned about your job security around here."

"Why's that?" he asks.

"Well, there seems to be a number of people in this restaurant encroaching on your job of taking care of us."

"I'm not sure I understand."

My wife shot me a look that was a clear warning not to go down that street.

"Never mind, we're good here."

"Excellent," John said. "I'll go see about those dinners."

When he had left, my wife said, "Really? Why do you have to act this way?"

"I was merely showing my concern about his status at the restaurant. Either he's incompetent and the other waitstaff is covering for him, or he's incredibly naïve about what's going on around here, with all these people after his job."

Before my better half could counter, our dinners arrived, delivered by, yet again, another person, whom I tagged as Tad for the purpose of our encounter and before releasing him back into the wild. My thinking was that Tad wanted to bring out our dishes to check out personally the scofflaw who forced a substitution. As our dinners hovered ambivalently over the table,

Tad asked, "Who has the baked stuffed shrimp, and who has the chicken Marsala?"

I asked, "Didn't John tell you? I knew he should have written it down instead of trying to remember everything, especially after our involved food preparation discussion."

My wife stopped any further damage by declaring she had ordered the chicken. After Tad placed the entrees in their appropriate places, he too dashed off. It was unclear whether he was escaping further inquisition on my part or the Reign of Terror at the next table.

At some point while dining on our meals, the prodigal son returned to ask, "How is everything?"

"Well, to be perfectly honest with you, John, besides the Haymarket Square Riot next door, I'm a little disappointed that we haven't seen more of you, seeing how you introduced yourself as the one 'taking care of us'." (I had intended for those last four words to be accompanied by the air quote salute, but did not include them in the actual conversation after catching a glimpse of my wife's face.) "Frankly, I was beginning to fear that you may have adopted us out to another server."

Evidently, John was still ignoring the same sarcasm that my wife wasn't, because he proceeded to explain that much of the service in this restaurant is a team effort, to ensure a more efficient dining experience. He then abruptly left to arbitrate a cease-fire across the way.

In support of John's explanation, the busboy of the team soon arrived to remove my wife's dinner plate. She had finished her meal long before me, seeing I had spent much of my 'dining experience' building bonds with the staff, and in the construction of a fortification made of substituted fries in the event the nearby civil war spread across the border. It was about this time that I wished I did have some of that sticky rice pilaf to serve as mortar between the fry planks for added strength and stability.

Eventually, someone, whom I guessed to be the designated nagger on the squad, stopped by our table, bowed in the direction of my entrée and asked, "Are you still working on that?" I believe it was at this point that my self-control governor stopped working and another of those endearing idiosyncrasies reared its ugly head.

"I'm sorry. Am I taking too long? You know that same question was asked of the artist, Alexandros of Antioch while working on his statue of Venus de Milo. I suppose he must have been too self-conscious to say 'no,' and look what we ended up with." Okay…none of those words actually left my mouth, because my dining partner for the evening, anticipating my snarky reply, lovingly nudged me under the table with her foot, which carried the unmistakable implication that I should be careful or I might choke on the next words to leave my talking-hole. So, what I actually said was, "No, thanks, I'm still working hard on it."

When I had finally finished, John, himself, appeared to remove my masterpiece.

"Will we be having any coffee, tea, or dessert tonight?"

I glanced over at my wife, whose face conveyed the clear message that her patience with me had already left the restaurant and was waiting in the car.

I said to John, "I'm thinking that would be a no for us, but I might suggest a potent bracer for yourself before having to crush the Boxer Rebellion over there."

I believe I actually saw John chuckle while placing the check on the table.

"Well, then I will leave this here for you. No rush. Take your…"

Before he could finish, I slapped my credit card down on the bill. I was not waiting around for the new terrorist nation, which was within spitting distance to us, to start mixing condiments and begin looking in our direction.

As we left the table, I managed a look back and swore I saw some WMDs amassed on the table from hell. Poor John. He thought he had it bad dealing with my rice pilaf. I wonder if exchanging mushroom clouds for mushrooms constitutes as a substitution.

This is why I believe restaurant waitstaff should be paid more than minimum wage. Many a time, they have to put up with unruly kids and on the rare occasion, a snarky patron.

Check please.

1984

Epistle to the Stalkers

My computer is spying on me. All these years I thought we had a professional and efficient symbiotic relationship. I inoculated it against viruses and protected it against electrical surges, and in return, it brought me all the amazing things there were to see in the world. So, I was deeply wounded to find out that it has been spilling its hard drive about me all over the World Wide Web. I'm sure it didn't start out that way, but over time, as the internet matured, websites became smarter and slicker. They soon learned to manipulate my computer, luring it deeper into their web with cookies, and storing personal things on it about me, such as the "thefuzzy1" password I use, or the brand of anti-fungal cream I once purchased. Once in their clutches, these sites distracted my computer with their fancy flash media, while they brainwashed its CPU using intricate JavaScript. The next thing I knew, IP address theft had taken place, and from then on, it was downhill. My computer is now under the control of others and giving me up at the drop of a PING.

As disheartening as this betrayal is to me, what really burns my CDs and has my hard drive in a defrag, is the unreserved commercialism of the internet, and the increasing lack of privacy we now have there. In an unabashed manner, every little detail of our lives is now stored and shared, becoming as transparent as the screens of our monitors.

After the commercial initialization of the internet in the 1980s, it wasn't long before this information superhighway became littered with ads that flashed and animated like signs on a Vegas strip, flickering us into epileptic seizures, all the while causing us to forget our original purpose in coming to the site. Then, when these websites felt that their blinking billboards were being ignored like so much white noise, they instructed their cunning web wizards to create ads that would unexpectedly pop up out of nowhere just like my Uncle Willie, whose nose whistled in a strangely hypnotic way as he talked. Some of these pop-ups erratically bobbed across your screen like those mysterious dark floaters in your eyes, and others aggressively followed as you scrolled down the web page. Annoyingly, many of these ads now explode into the forefront just as the page you are seeking loads, refusing to allow you entrance to the site until you have searched the entire ad at great length for the atomic-sized X to close it out.

It seems that many of the programs and websites today want you to store your videos, eBooks, and work files in a place called the "Cloud." Now perhaps you're more organized than me, but I know that it can sometimes be a labor of Hercules to find stuff in my own desk, never mind in some ethereal warehouse along with everybody else's stuff. Occasionally, my files are stored there by accident, like the time I discovered that this Cloud was the default setting for a particular program I used. The next time I tried to retrieve that file—in fact, this very essay—it was nowhere to be found, mysteriously lost in the Cloud, leaving me to wonder—a happenstance or by design? Later, as I was fastidiously attempting to recreate the work in this misplaced file, my faithful computer dinged that I had a new email message from the Cloud, which read something like this:

> *Good news! Your lost file has been located! It was found under a discredited Wikipedia entry. Unfortunately, it appears that something with the consistency and coloration of a hazelnut macchiato has been spilled on it. For your inconvenience, we have automatically upgraded your account and have allotted you an extra 5 GB of prime storage area right next to the NSA bin. If you have any questions, please feel free to contact our supervisor, the Sky. Thank you for saving with the Cloud.*

Although incredibly intrusive and revealing to the point of exploitation, social media sites, while not entirely blameless in their complicity, do rely upon the private, and many times frivolous contributions of willing participants, eager to post every fatuous factoid of their lives. To these people, I would like to say:

Please believe me when I say that I honestly don't care to know that your mother-in-law's best friend Hazel's favorite Elvis song is "Adam and Evil," or that your day started "really sucky" because the Honey Nut Cheerios you were craving all night long had been put back on the shelf empty. Also, there's something rather disconcerting and more than just a little bit creepy that 756 people—mostly total strangers—"Like" the photo of your two-year-old's naked tush, while only 8 feel the same way about the breathtakingly stunning photograph you captured of the sun setting over the Sierra Nevada range. So in 140 characters or less, I ask you—doesn't recording every single deed you do, or every vacuous thought you have, smack a little of self-important arrogance and just a tad extravagant? (I guess that was a few characters over—I probably shouldn't have used the words vacuous and arrogance).

On top of all this, anyone with a cell phone camera can capture and depict you in any mortifyingly awkward situation, making you the unwilling victim on these very same platforms or any of those video web sites where it seems the integrity of humanity and its intellectual underbelly is exposed on a daily basis.

For these and other reasons, I have thus far eschewed membership in any of these platforms. Although, a couple of years ago, I accidentally did join one of those networking sites, when someone I barely knew from my old job sent me an email stating that he, "would like to add me to his professional network." I deleted this request the first two times thinking that maybe I was being robo-spammed. But after it arrived a third time, practically begging me to join him, I relented, fearing that I would somehow be personally insulting him if I didn't respond. So I joined, even though my employment status would read as "recently retired" and I am no longer a professional in any network nexus or ganglia. I rarely log onto the site and my lack of participation, even if I knew what to do—which I don't—is supported by the fact that my profile contains only my name and lists my geographic designation as the United States. Oddly, even though I don't remember doing it, the only other item on my site is a picture of me in New Orleans holding a map and looking up at a life-sized, bronze statue of Ignatius Reilly— protagonist from *A Confederacy of Dunces*—as if I were soliciting him on how to get to Bubba Gump's Shrimp Restaurant. As you can tell by this description, this is not exactly a profile of legend and light-years away from being a professional resume builder. Yet somehow, through the miracle of the internet's twisty tendrils, I have now been linked or connected to 228 corporate ladder climbers along the eastern seaboard and one concrete manufacturer in Guam.

It has become a common practice of many of the large websites to track our window shopping as we stroll around the world wide mall, so they can effectively target their ads or promotions to our determined tastes—or so they claim. As an example, I was researching different sites on medical alert systems for my elderly aunt, and am now bombarded with ads for bariatric briefs, pill organizers, and suggestions that I might also benefit from uplift seating or pressure relief mattresses. All of which, I do admit though, sound pretty cool.

Even more disconcerting to my growing sensation of paranoia was my last visit to a website I frequent when I'm stuck on a crossword clue. Suddenly, there in the upper corner of the page was an ad that scrolled up in a small box. It was for a popular footwear E-tailer, whom for anonymous purposes I'll call Sole Brothers. Even though I had visited them only once in the past, I still figured that I would probably be targeted with their advertisements sometime during my future surfing. However, I was not prepared for the ad's content as it appeared on this crossword site. It read:

> *Thomas, please come back to Sole Brothers. We miss you and you left some items on your wish list—SoleBrothers.com.*

I was stunned. Not only had they sent an ad, but it was personalized and not just with my name, but with the fact that I had obviously forgotten to finish my shopping at their "store." Keep in mind that these were items merely on my wish list. Even if they were in my "shopping cart," I'm still not under any obligation to purchase them. I mean, who among us, at one time or another, has not deftly left a real-life shopping cart laden with goodies by the aisle's wayside upon suddenly realizing that our wallet was remotely located at home on the top of the dresser? This wasn't even the Sole Brother's security hounding me because I had failed to put my unclaimed items from my shopping cart back on their e-shelves. No, these items were just on my wish list, perhaps best thought of as a retail bucket list. I'd like to be able to say to them, *first, how in hell did you find me here on this crossword site? Has someone been following me since I left your store? Secondly, are my wishes honestly taking up that much space in your hard drive store? If so, might I suggest just storing them in the Cloud, and I'll get back to you about them.*

It should be fairly clear by now that I am an individual with personal space and privacy issues. The final invasion of my privacy, which so frosted my cookies and thus prompted this rant, occurred just the other day. In my sad attempt at writing humor, I submit pieces to various magazines, both off and online. As it should be, I always try to match the writing with the magazine's particular content. In this business, sometimes you make a match and they publish it, or you don't and they reject it. Then again, sometimes the myopic editors with their freakishly little heads are too unsophisticated to recognize the droll, cerebral wordplay and concepts you have sent them, rife with mirthful comparative and contrasting embellishments, and so they unceremoniously give them the old heave-ho. Obviously, this was not the case with the enlightened editors who published this essay.

I keep a list of all these magazines in my browser's bookmarks and constantly refer to them. For the purposes of describing this last coup de grace to my privacy, I am going to disguise the names of the two magazines involved, so as not to draw the attention of the internet police to the real publications, thus keeping open the possibilities of my being published in either or both of them in the near future. On this particular day of interest, I had opened up the submissions page of *The Trumpet's Soliloquy* to review their guidelines and content. I must interject here to note that I had never previously corresponded with this magazine in any way, other than to scan its submissions page. However, when the page appeared on my screen, right there in glaringly yellow text, poised above the regular title "Submit to *The Trumpet's Soliloquy*," were these words: "Because *Finian's Whiskey-Breath Review* rejected you…". I instantly whipped my head around to see who was looking over my shoulder! What the hell? How could this have happened? How could this magazine have known that I had a humor piece rejected by *Finian's*? Immediately, I searched for both magazines on Google to see if they were somehow related through either marriage or subsidy. That would at least partially explain this uninvited infringement into my private affairs. After an exhaustive investigation, I could find no connection whatsoever, but now find myself the unlucky recipient of a spate of advertisements for marching band instruments and Gaelic whiskeys.

Following this last episode, I wanted so badly to quit using the internet to get away from this persistent spying. After a brief cooling off period, I realized that I would not be able to resist the siren-like allure of the World Wide Web with its vast informative and supportive websites. After all, who could resist websites such as *InmatesForYou.com*, a site that matches you up with that perfect felon after a required waiting period, or *neuticles.com*, where you can buy implanted cosmetic testicles for your spayed dog to ease his embarrassment with the other good boys. I swear to you those are actual sites. You simply cannot miss out on things like that.

Besides, by now it was clearly evident that my digital DNA had been scattered all over the information superhighway like a messy car wreck. These commercial enterprises already had their assertive big foot in the front door, and the best I could hope for now is that they don't let my nose-whistling Uncle Willie squeeze inside.

Surviving the Cure

Epistle to the Transgressors

The following piece first appeared in the online magazine, Hobo Pancakes. No shit, I'm not making that up. That's its real name. Look it up.

In the movie *Butch Cassidy and the Sundance Kid*, there is a scene in which the two main characters are cornered high on a cliff overlooking a raging river, and their only escape is to jump into the water far below. The usually confident Sundance is more than a little reluctant to take the plunge, and when pressed by Butch, finally confesses, "I can't swim." Butch pauses and then says, "Why you crazy bastard, the fall will probably kill you!"

Regrettably, this seems to be the same scenario with the pharmaceuticals we take. They may help us to "escape" the ailment we have, but their side effects could end up causing us more harm than the illness itself.

If you have ever suffered through the searing torment of weekday, daytime television, from the early morning hours until just after the Final Jeopardy question—the time when most seniors exit the demographic viewing pool—then you've witnessed those endless ads for medications. They are ubiquitous during those time slots and pretty much follow the same three-part script. In the opening scene, we are given an introduction to a gloomy, despairing, embarrassing, debilitating, or uncomfortable physical condition. In the second part, the cheery, hopeful doctor or the overbearing, meddlesome neighbor or friend informs you about the remedial properties of some new wonder drug. Both these parts occur within the first fifteen seconds of the commercial. The majority of the remaining time is taken up by the final part, which presents a laundry list of disclaimers and side effects included by the legal departments of the major pharmaceutical companies.

Now I understand why this is done, but what is most unnerving is not only the length of the list of possible side effects, but the severity of health risks they pose individually or collectively. Without question, many of these risks carry far greater consequences than the actual disorder they are meant to alleviate. This is why these commercials always end with the warning: *before taking this product, always consult with your physician or mortician—whichever comes first.*

Of course, these risks are intended to be precautionary warnings and affect only a small percentage of patients, but the sobering reality is that someone, sometime, or somehow, developed one of these side effects, or how else would they be known? As further proof, just look at the overabundance of ambulance-chasing, law firm ads, soliciting calls from victims suffering from the side effects of these drugs.

By way of example, I will now use a medication of mine and list its stated possible side effects. Even though the list is mind-numbingly long, I'm afraid you are going to have to put up with it. After all, I am tinkering with the HIPAA privacy policy by exposing my personal medical condition to you. I will not specifically identify the drug or the pharmaceutical company involved, even though they freely delineate these risks ad nauseam in their own ads, websites, and on the products themselves. I just don't want those deep pockets coming after me.

The drug of note is a NSAID (non-steroidal anti-inflammatory drug) used primarily to treat rheumatoid arthritis or ankylosing spondylitis. The possible "light," or as I've seen some medications call them, "bothersome" side effects are: (*my personal comments will be the ones in parentheses*) constipation, diarrhea (*could possibly be the wonder drug that causes and cures all in one pill*), dizziness, gas, headaches, heartburn, upset stomach, and stuffy nose. I can live with most of these as long as the medication does what it is meant to do—although the constipation and diarrhea could be a real pain in the ass.

What follows now is a catalog of the more serious side effects: severe allergic reactions such as rash, hives, itching, trouble breathing, and swelling of the mouth, face, lips, or tongue. Bloody or black tarry stools (*this one is especially unsettling if you have also exhibited one particular" bothersome" effect listed above*), change in the amount of urine produced (*this might not be such a bad thing, as it could cut down on my adult diaper cost. Okay, I've just divulged another of my medical circumstances—so keep on reading*). Confusion (*and just how will I recognize this?*), dark urine (*to be paired with red meats, pastas, and strong cheeses*), depression (*no kidding!*), fainting, fast or irregular heartbeat, fever, chills, or persistent sore throat, hearing loss, mental or mood changes, numbness of arm or leg, one-sided weakness, red, swollen, blistered or peeling skin. Ringing in the ears (*will not be detected if suffering from the hearing loss side effect*), seizures, severe headaches, or dizziness, severe or persistent stomach pain or nausea, severe vomiting, shortness of breath, sudden or unexplained weigh gain (*it's the meds, honest!*). Swelling of hands, legs or feet, unusual bruising or bleeding, unusual joint or muscle pain (*now keep in mind those are two of the symptoms that prompted the use of this drug in the first place*). Unusual tiredness or weakness, vision or speech changes (*I now speak fluent Uzbek*), vomit that looks like coffee grounds (*which describes any given Sunday morning after a raucous Saturday night*), yellowing of the skin or eyes (*sounding a bit jaundice to me*).

Then lastly, but most definitely not least, is this beauty: may increase chance of heart attack or stroke that can lead to death. This chance increases if you have heart disease (*whoa…whoa…whoa, back it up— beep, beep, beep—can lead to death? I didn't sign on for this. I just wanted those old aches and pains relieved!*) or risk factors for it, such as high blood pressure, or if taken for long periods (*I have been ingesting this—what now appears to be a death pill—for approximately fifteen to twenty years. Is that considered a long period?*)

Are you kidding me? The inventory of possible side effects for this drug alone reads like the top ten maladies on the World Health Organization's most wanted list. I mean, it goes from constipation to death in one commercial. After hearing all this, tell me, who in their right mind would voluntarily opt to take this medication? As a fairly, rational person, I would expect to receive from this drug what it was primarily intended to do and not rheumatoid arthritis pain relief with a side order of apocalyptic pestilence. I imagine even Socrates would have blanched at this logic. *Socks, here's your hemlock. Now, in the few minutes it will take to kill you, you might experience mood changes or a ringing in your ears. Just so you know.*

Imagine if everyday food items, like, say Oreos®, came with a possible side effects warning as well. *Eating of this delectable sandwich cookie may cause a rise in gluten levels, an increase in hyperactivity—especially in children, a craving for cold milk, and unusual swelling in the butt or stomach areas, an unnatural impulse to twist things apart leading to separation anxieties. Severe increase in sugar levels in diabetics or may cause the onset of Type 2 adult diabetes, poor eating habits that can lead to milk spraying from nose—which could lead to death by choking or embarrassment.*

The NSAID I just described is just one of the medications I am currently involved with. Similar side effects are repeated with these other drugs, but some new ones noted on the labels are: irreversible damage to the retina of the eye, twitching or uncontrolled movement (*which describes my dance form to a T*). Loss of balance or coordination (*ditto the previous*), light sensitivity, seeing halos around lights, pale skin (*all trendy, vampiric traits*), and unusual thoughts or behavior (*which just happens to be my core affliction according to my family and friends*).

Apparently, another side effect of many drugs is that you have a diminished capacity to operate heavy equipment, which in and of itself, is a bit misleading and relative in nature. Just what is considered as heavy equipment? Are they talking about a jackhammer or a M1A1 Abrams tank—neither of which I can effectively handle even without the meds.

Then there are those disclaimers, which give one pause to wonder why they are even there in the first place, such as the one that warns, *for erections lasting longer than four hours, please consult your physician.* I don't think I'm out of line here by stating that I believe this to be the exact purpose of the drug. In fact, maybe they should be charging extra for such an added benefit. That's like an aspirin company stating, *for periods without a headache lasting longer than four hours please consult your doctor.* This begs another question. Why exactly are you consulting your doctor about a marathon stiffy? What's he going to do, whack it with a ruler? You could self-medicate with that one.

The obvious dilemma at hand is that after hearing the litany of adverse secondary effects, do we still want to risk taking the drug or would we rather live with the ailment we already have and know? I suppose the answer lies in the nature and gravity of the disease. Up until I arrived at upper, upper middle age, I even hated taking an aspirin into my mortal coil. However, once I reached the AARP zone, all those things I had previously ignored, suddenly became cause célèbre for a new medication.

Even now, I still try to rebel and continually ask my physicians if I really need to keep tethering myself to these drugs. I express my concern over all the side effects and how they make me feel as if I'm playing Russian roulette on a daily basis. However, they all reassure me that the dosage I am on is not that high and as long as I get this or that checked out regularly, I should be fine. I suppose they must convince most of us, because we continue to take these medications. Knowing the enemy that we have, over the ones we do not have and may not even come down with, is further inducement.

By the way, in case you didn't recall the movie scene referred to at the beginning of this piece, the Sundance Kid does jump and survives the fall. Therefore, I imagine I will stay the course with the meds, but I'll be keeping that 1-800-NASTY MED law firm number on speed dial.

I need to stop now, because writing about this is giving me a whale of a headache, and I haven't had one of those for hours. I'm not sure, but I think I was supposed to call someone if that happened. Then again, I could be suffering from confusion and unusual thoughts.

Wildlife Strife

Epistle to St. Francis of Assisi

This is a pathetically sad tale of frustration, guilt, and incompetence. Hope you enjoy it.

So how do you get rid of a pest? Not the two-legged kind, like Neighbor Dave, whose built-in radar targets me whenever I so much as step outside my house for any reason, and upon whom, nothing short of a high-voltage cattle prod or a restraining order has had much effect. No, by pest, I'm referring to some of our fellow organic inhabitants with whom we share the earth, and more specifically, our yards and sometimes even our living quarters.

On a personal level, I find it very difficult to visit harm upon other living things sporting less than six legs—with the notable exceptions being some pit bulls, and of course, Neighbor Dave. However, when subject to my wife's urgent pleas to do something to stop the floral carnage in her garden, I can be driven to measures beyond my comfort zone. This all comes from the same woman who urgently alerts me whenever any insect is found inside our home—her personal no-fly zone.

Therefore, it is I, who must bloody his hands to get rid of whatever the menace may be. Still, as previously stated, I don't really have an issue doing the dirty deed on insects, spiders, and their ilk. It's when it starts moving up the class taxonomy ladder that my biological remorse sets in.

My self-affirmed justification in eliminating these pests is based upon the argument that these uninvited guests are the invaders, and I am merely protecting my turf. This is further supported by the Prime Directive of my personal system of biological ethics, which states: *humans and pets inside, and all other creatures, along with Neighbor Dave outside.* Obviously, the fact that we don't own any pets simplifies this rule for me.

During some cold winters, mice will often test this rule by attempting to take up residency in our home. Whenever that happens, I usually wait until I hear scratching in the wall, spot one squirting across the floor, or find my Cheerios box perforated at the bottom, before setting down the mousetraps. Unfortunately, this has been the only method to solve this problem successfully. Scaring or trying to reason with them is fruitless. Glue traps are a mess and must totally fray the nerves of any mice stuck in place. The mousetraps have proven to be effective and more humane than other methods. They usually eliminate the mice indoors and probably intimidate any remaining ones, forcing them back outside and away from my electrical wires, Cheerios, and wife.

There are occasions, however, when there's a problem with the traps. For instance, I might run across a Mensa mouse that somehow has figured out how to strip the peanut butter bait from the trap without triggering it. In such a case, it usually just requires a bit more ingenuity and peanut butter to capture this escape artist. This is typically accomplished by slathering on copious amounts of the bait and working it well into the catch of the trap, so Chuck E. Cheese needs to poke around a bit harder, thereby sealing his fate.

In another instance, the mouse actually took off with the trap. When I went down into the basement to check on its status, I discovered that the trap had vanished and was nowhere to be found. Let me tell you, a thing like that, can strike fear into your heart. First, I'm thinking this must be one powerful rodent to perform such a feat, and second, just what in hell is he going to do with it?

I've caught the majority of invading mice in our basement, where I'm sure they're making their way in from some crevice to the outside. However, there was one particular mouse that prowled around in the attic. At night, as we lay in bed, we could hear him scuffling across the floorboards right above our heads, doing who knows what mischievous mouse things. Hell, it might even be the very one that absconded with the trap in the basement and was now plotting some kind of payback for us the next time we went up to the attic. Obviously, this could not be allowed to happen and so this mouse had to go.

I set a trap near some of our girls' old toys, this being the area where we heard most of the sounds coming from. That same night, my wife and I were awakened by the most horrific noise coming from above. This was no pitter-patter of little mice feet. This was a loud thumping sound as if something heavy was being dragged across the attic floor.

As the reluctant, but appointed protector of the manor, I was in charge of investigating this sinister and possibly threatening disturbance. Armed with a baseball bat, crucifix and silver blade (nail file) I headed for the attic, seemingly prepared to face any evil that crossed my path. As quietly as possible, I opened the door to the attic, and noiselessly started up the stairs, all the while hoping that pajamas and bare feet would not be to my disadvantage. However, it was at this point, I realized that my efforts for staging a strike using the element of surprise would be thwarted, when I had to flip on the attic light to see where I was going. On the other hand, I was partially relieved that I was not about to be bushwhacked by whatever entity with infrared vision awaited me in the darkness above.

Upon reaching the attic floor and scanning the perimeter, I spied neither monster nor any nefarious movement of any kind. There were also no longer any sinister noises other than my own shallow breaths. I felt somewhat comforted that whatever was up here wasn't larger than me in size, or I would have already seen it. Still, I remained wary of the possibility of that whole sharp teeth thing.

Cautiously, I moved towards the approximate area where we had heard the clatter. Approaching the toy storage section where I had set the trap, I spotted something directly in my path. There, staring up at me with eerie, lifeless eyes was a Cabbage Patch Kid, a once highly sought after doll of girlhood avarice, but now relegated to the status of a "well-that-was-then" artifact.

I thought it odd and more than a little disturbing that this doll was lying alone in the middle of the floor. But when it started moving towards me, I nearly lost it. It would move a little, stop, and then move again. Regaining my composure, I quickly rationalized the situation as being of two possibilities. Either we had a poltergeist in the attic, or little Eberta Juliette had become possessed by a demon.

After the doll moved again, and I had issued a high-pitched, girly scream, I witnessed the third possibility. There, peeking out of Eberta Juliette's long, golden locks was a mouse! As I moved in for a closer inspection, the mouse abruptly scooted under the hair, and the doll began moving away from me. Grabbing the doll, I turned it over, expecting Mickey to hightail it to parts unknown, but there he was, ensnarled in the doll's hair along with the mousetrap.

Apparently what happened was, when the trap sprung, it snared some of the doll's tresses, cushioning the mouse from the trap's hammer, but entangling it along with the mousetrap, which allowed the mouse to take little Eberta on a joyride across the attic floor and thus creating the ruckus we had heard.

Believing the mouse had endured enough stress and had earned its freedom, I carried the whole mass of confusion downstairs, ignoring my wife's urgent, "Well, what was it?" I deemed the explanation too involved to get into at that moment. Once outside, I carefully cut the mouse loose of the yarn hair, and watched it swiftly run off—free and with a tale to tell.

Unfortunately, it didn't end as well for poor Eberta Juliette. Due to Operation Freedom, she lost quite a bit of hair on one side of her head, ensuring a lifetime of unconscionable chiding and snubbing in the Cabbage Patch.

Unlike the mice, we normally did not have issues with the neighborhood squirrels. They were happy to cavort about outside, and we were happy to let them do their squirrely thing. However, there was one notable exception. It was a Saturday morning and I was reading the newspaper in the family room. I thought I had heard some rustling sounds coming from the living room. At first, I passed it off as nothing, but when it happened again, I decided to investigate.

My experience told me to first check the fireplace for a bird that might have become trapped inside, seeing this had happened once before at our previous residence. Looking through the glass doors and screen, I didn't see anything, and thought that if left alone, the bird might find its own way out. So I returned to the family room.

Soon, the rustling began again, but it was now sounding more frantic. I had to do something before the poor bird injured itself. This time, when I checked the fireplace, I saw the trapped varmint wasn't a bird after all. Somehow, a small squirrel had managed to make its way past the chimney cap and descend into our fireplace.

Figuring that it wouldn't be able to climb back up, I viewed my only option as opening the fireplace doors to give it a way out. Not wanting the thing to bolt out, running amok throughout the house causing untold havoc and unbridled screaming, I first opened the front door, which was opposite the fireplace. I'm fairly certain I was relying on some false notion that animals can sense the outdoors and freedom, and when afforded the opportunity would make their way lickety-split along the most direct route. However, just in case I was wrong, I explained to my wife what the plan was, and waited while she packed a bag to move in with friends until the operation was over.

With the coast now cleared, I stood back and opened the glass doors and screens. Nothing happened. Nothing spurted out in a mad dash towards emancipation. I ventured a look inside the fireplace, and didn't see the little fellow anywhere. Thinking that it must be terrified and hiding somewhere in there, I stole out of the living room to afford it open passage.

I watched from the family room, but there was still no breakout happening. After several minutes, I reentered the living room to assess the situation. As I did, suddenly, a small gray blur of fur sped across the living room floor in front of me and out the front door. I barely had time to witness it scale the outside of the house and head up towards the roof. I was relieved the situation was resolved without any loss of life or home goods, but a bit uneasy that Rocket J. Squirrel had just headed back up to where his distressing adventure all began. Not confident in his short-term memory skills, I immediately made sure that the damper was securely closed. Next time, he would have to find his own way out.

With this one exception, the other squirrels were content to remain outdoors gathering nuts and scurrying around.

Oddly, there was yet another event involving our chimney cap, which, for some reason, had become a beacon for the wildlife in our yard. For years, we have had a woodpecker living in the maple tree behind the house, and but for some rat-a-tat-tatting on occasion, we had co-existed as good neighbors in peaceful harmony. Then one year, something happened to disturb that tranquility. During breakfast one morning, we heard a strange tinny vibration that seemed to be coming from somewhere within the house. It would last for three or four seconds and then just as abruptly stop. This would repeat itself several more times, before finally stopping altogether. We couldn't figure out what could be making this metallic sound. Over the next few days, we continued to hear the same sound around the same time each morning. I finally determined the sound could be heard clearer and louder near the fireplace. I didn't think the cause of the noise was an animal because it was too rhythmic and mechanical. When the vibration started up again, it sounded too distant and had to be coming from outside the house.

While standing in the front yard, I faced the house and shaded my eyes from the sun. Looking up at the top of the chimney I spotted our good neighbor, the woodpecker, perched atop the chimney cap. Every ten seconds or so, it would begin riveting on the metal cover. I have no idea why I then shouted, "Knock it off!" being fully aware that this particular bird didn't speak any English, but I hoped it at least understood the nuance of an angry tone. Apparently, it did, because it promptly flew away. Regrettably, this same approach never worked on our other neighbor, Dave.

I'm not sure why the woodpecker was doing this. Perhaps it was merely sharpening its power tool or maybe sending a message to distant relatives. Whatever the reason, I was fairly certain that all that drilling couldn't be good for the cap. After a few more days of his drum solos and my chasing him off, he suddenly stopped coming around, either having accomplished what he had set out to do, or realizing that the tinnitus in his head wasn't worth the trouble.

The only serious episode we ever had with an animal intruder, involved what I surmised to be a raccoon, which had become trapped inside our garage all night. We had returned home late one evening, and noticed we had forgotten to close one of the garage doors upon leaving earlier that night. Without realizing an animal lay hunkered down somewhere inside, I closed the garage door and headed off to bed.

At some point the next day, I walked into the garage from the breezeway. The scene I came upon can best be described as the aftermath of a bad bar fight. Items were knocked off benches and walls everywhere. It looked like everything that could be overturned or spilled was just that.

I quickly recognized that this had to have been the work of a trapped, desperate animal in a mad panic to find its way out. At the same time, I also realized that whatever had committed all this mayhem was still inside with me. Suddenly terrified, I envisioned some frazzled, rabid creature with bloodshot eyes and nerves frayed thin, crouching nearby and far beyond anxious to shred me to tatters with claws sharply honed from a long night of digging and scratching. So, the first thing I did was to open both garage doors before the concealed varmint decided that I, too, was fair game. I then went into the house to give the animal time to evacuate the premises safely.

An hour later, I returned to the crime scene, genuinely hoping that I was now alone in the garage. Seeing no sudden movements of escape, I began assessing the damage. Garden pots lay in shards on the floor and the rubber weather-stripping was torn away from the bottom of one of the garage doors. Cans, boxes, and tools, which had been on shelves, hooks, and cabinets, were now strewn all over the place, like so much damage after a bad storm. It was such a disaster that I was even tempted to call FEMA, hoping they might spring for part of the cleanup.

Paw prints covered both cars and were clearly noticeable on the windows of the garage doors. The raccoon (the paw prints now confirmed this) must have stood on the trunk of the cars and pressed on the garage windows. There was even evidence that our prisoner had visited the loft above the cars, knocking down some stored items from up there as well. Worse still, there were feces and urine everywhere, in what I hoped was only a testimony to the animal's state of fright and not him trying to mark new territory.

Eventually, I got the whole nightmare cleaned up, vowing to never again leave the garage doors open when leaving the house. As an added precaution before closing them for the night, I now bark like a dog to scare off any animal intruders that might be lurking inside. I know that sounds a little silly, but ever since I've employed this tactic, we've had no further home invasions. And despite a couple of animal control complaints about the barking noises—filed against us by some anonymous neighbor—it was still worth it. So suck on that, Dave.

By far, the most frustrating situation with pests occurred this past summer in our backyard, and in particular, my wife's flower gardens, because they had become the playgrounds of a band of merry chipmunks. Now personally, I have nothing against those cute critters, having been blissfully entertained as a toon-viewing kid by the likes of Chip and Dale, and Alvin and his brothers. However, I also know from watching those cartoons that they can be more than a little mischievous from time to time—well, maybe most of the time. Still, they generally left me alone, never once tying my shoelaces together or dumping a bucket of acorns on my head.

What I failed to realize—but which was quickly pointed out to me by my wife—was how destructive the chipmunks could be in the garden. To start with, there was the extensive excavation of a tunnel system which ran under the gardens, rock wall, and sidewalks, and which had so many conveniently located points of access that it would have put most major metropolitans' subway systems to shame. We more or less, ignored them the first year of their tenancy in an," aw-they're-so-cute" sort of way. However, this year with more of the flowers suffering from the "munchies," and the chipmunks displaying a more brazen disregard towards our reasonable requests to "cut that out," we knew we had to rid ourselves of their adorable presence.

Unfortunately, at the same time Alvin and Company were up to their shenanigans, a woodchuck took up residency somewhere under our hedges along the side of the yard. As with the chipmunks, we put up with its cuteness for one summer before it too, went over to the dark side this year. It had become quite comfortable with strolling about the lawn and making short work of many varieties of blossoms in the garden, depending on its taste du jour. Therefore, it would also have to go.

Now, if for any reason, you ever have need to mention you have a pest infestation at your home to a friend, co-worker, or a Neighbor Dave, be prepared to receive a medley of "tried and true" home remedies for addressing your pest problem, along with countless "funny" personal anecdotes involving similar pests. Both of which, you will find neither helpful or amusing in any context.

Our first plan of attack involved the use of cayenne pepper spray on the plants to discourage their consumption by both chipmunks and woodchuck alike. We quickly discovered that not only was this ineffective, but both pests seem to regard this "deterrent" more like a condiment for their meal, while only occasionally seeking relief with water from the birdbath.

We had no better success with the mothballs we scattered about the garden terrain and near their holes. In fact, the next day, we found them moved all over the place as if the chipmunks had enjoyed some version of rodent miniature golf. The woodchuck just seemed to use them as palate cleansers between floral courses.

Recognizing that I had a lot of success with mousetraps indoors, I thought they might do the trick outside with the chipmunks. After all, they're just mice with stripes, right? I baited the traps with peanut butter and then stuck on some sunflower seeds to sweeten the pot further. Later, upon checking them, I discovered the first trap stripped clean without having been triggered, while the second one was snapped shut, but with no chipmunk or bait anywhere to be seen. It appeared that chipmunks were cleverer than mice. So this tactic was out.

The next approach resulted from a search on the internet and was claimed by many to be effective in dealing with "the chipmunk problem." I set up a pail filled with water and laid a plank of wood from the ground to the top of the pail. Sunflower seeds led up the angled board as an invitation to the chipmunks to walk the plank up to the rim of the bucket. Once there they would view more seeds floating on the water, acting as an enticement to take the plunge; all the while hoping the furry little critters would fail to remember they didn't know the first thing about swimming.

Once that system was set up, I then tackled dealing with the woodchuck. I borrowed a Havahart© trap from a friend in which to ensnare the old whistle pig. As bait, I used some watermelon rinds, on which I smeared some peanut butter and topped it off with a dash of sunflower seeds (a recipe since borrowed by a local health food restaurant).

With my defenses now armed, and the lawn looking more like an obstacle course for animals rather than a backyard, I was ready to do battle.

Although probably predictable, the results were nothing short of a total failure. The chipmunks ate all the sunflower seeds leading up to the brim of the pail, but then retreated. They returned a little later though with what looked like rafts made of sticks held together by peanut butter. After paddling around the pail scooping up the floating sunflower seeds, they then entertained themselves by playing with moth "beach" balls. Not yet having had their fill of fun, they next went on a raid to the woodchuck trap to safely nosh on the seeds and peanut butter in there, being too light to spring the door shut.

Not discouraged, I restocked the Havahart© trap, but this time with some seedless watermelon, knowing that the chipmunks wouldn't bother with that. In no time at all, I caught a squirrel. I promptly released him on his own recognizance since our quarrel was not with him, seeing that we had already settled our differences over past matters.

On the other front, while we did not hold out much hope for success, we left the pail and plank in place, refreshing the water and seeds from time to time.

My next strategy was to change the bait I had been using for the woodchuck. Hearing from someone that they liked cantaloupe, I placed a few fresh, juicy slices inside the trap. Yet, upon my next check, the cantaloupes had somehow been removed from the metal cage without triggering the trap. They were also pretty much gnawed down to their rinds. This same scenario was visited upon me two more times.

The backyard combat had now been raging for well over a week, and not only were the animals winning, but were rubbing my nose in it as well. And to make matters worse, my friend, who had lent me his Havahart© trap, called to see if he could get it back, as he himself, had a woodchuck eating his tomato plants. By now, I thought I could use a little cease fire in the war, so I delivered the trap to him that afternoon. The next day, he called to tell me he was returning the trap to me, having already caught his poacher with some watermelon and released it into the wild. While I was happy for his quick success, it only increased my own feeling of incompetence. I was minimally consoled, by telling myself that perhaps I just had the smartest pests in town congregating in my yard.

With the battle renewed, and my determination rekindled, I loaded the trap again, but this time with three cantaloupe slices and two half ears of corn. This time, I decided to place the trap right next to the side hedges, where I believed the woodchuck's lair to be.

Early the next morning, when I looked out the upstairs window into the backyard, I immediately noticed the trap door was closed! I hurriedly got myself dressed so I could take the trap and its captive on their long overdue trip to the woods, where I would release him into his natural habitat to become Mother Nature's problem.

On my way outside, I stopped by the garage to pop my trunk and lay down some plastic in case the woodchuck in his frightened state suddenly shit the bed, so to speak. Just before heading outside, I grabbed a blanket to cover the cage to ease the nervousness of the woodchuck and to be in full compliance with the Geneva Conventions.

Strutting my Big White Hunter walk towards the trap, I had a feeling of relief and perhaps a little bit of sadness that this long battle with my formidable foe was finally coming to an end. But when I was near enough to see inside the cage, what I saw staring back at me were not the cute, sappy eyes of a woodchuck, but the dark, masked ones of a raccoon! I stopped fast in my tracks. I didn't even know this player was in the game.

The collateral damage among the other species in my neighborhood was quickly mounting. I wondered, how was it I could catch the purportedly clever raccoon, but not the *dumb-dee-dumb* woodchuck? Overshadowing all of these thoughts was this one: If this guy has rabies, I have a much bigger problem on my hands than woodchucks or chipmunks.

Despite all this head mash going on inside me, I screwed up the courage to release the raccoon. I hoped that he didn't turn on me in a pissed-off, fit-of-rabid rage, and shred my lower torso to bloody strips of flesh, all the while infusing me with a virus which had insanity written all over it and headed straight for my brain.

Mercifully, it scampered off, leaving behind a pile of dirt where it had tried to dig its way out of the trap, along with some soil-encrusted cantaloupe slices. I didn't see the corn anywhere, and assumed it had been eaten during the raccoon's long night of captivity. However, two days later, a stripped corncob suddenly reappeared on top of the mound of dirt where the trap had been.

This was all getting to be too much. The animals were now making sport of me. The woodchuck was taunting me with its Houdini escape acts; the 45-rpm giggles of the chipmunks could be heard reverberating throughout their subterranean maze, and now a raccoon, whom I set free, mind you, was outwardly mocking me by returning his scraps to the scene of the crime.

As I write this now, I am looking out my office window at the ineffectual bucket trap and the Havahart© cage, impotently laden with a fresh supply of cantaloupe. With these pests eluding my every effort, and with me having reached both the end of my patience and fresh produce, I did what any rational person would do in such a desperate situation. I called the Acme Company and ordered one large metal safe, specially designed for dropping from great heights onto unsuspecting prey. Now, before any of you call PETA on me, I want you to know that I would never go Wile E. Coyote on those poor animals. No, I'm saving this baby for Neighbor Dave.

Author's Note:
For the record, Neighbor Dave is a fictional character I contrived to represent the stereotypical, pesky, next door neighbor who irritates the shit out of you. During the time frame of this animal fiasco, I had no actual neighbors named Dave that I was aware of. Although after finishing this book, it occurred to me that this could change at any time, and someone named Dave might actually move into the neighborhood. So, if that happens—along with the extremely rare possibility that he should read this book—I would like to apologize in advance about this unintentional association. Furthermore, please feel free to send over any of your friends so I can fully exonerate you.

The Game of Greed

Epistle to the Insatiable
To Karl and Friedrich: I think they would have approved.

Throughout this book, most of my grumblings have been light-hearted, hopefully somewhat amusing, and taken with either a grain of salt or a habanero seed, depending on your partiality. They have covered topics which most of society—at least the well-adjusted members—would consider trivial or bothersome itches and tolerated as such. However, there are times–this being one of them—when I need to get down-and-dirty serious because there simply isn't a way to find anything humorous about the subject, either because it is too heinous an offense or too morally corrupt, and probably both. I preface this rant to prepare you for the somber tale of helplessness, frustration, and anger that follows.

First, an Introduction of Sorts

A little greed isn't really such a bad thing despite the fact that its company includes the six other Deadly Sins. With the exception of certain monks and Warren Buffet, we all give into its lure once in a while. Usually, it involves only a modest amount of innocent gluttony. However, greed can easily become a problem if it gets out of hand, turns malicious, and causes harm to others.

Throughout history, nations have been built upon the

foundation of greed for land, power, and wealth. However, over time, this controlled greed tends to become more unrestrained. When this happens, things start to go wrong and regimes are forced into changes. Governments are fragile systems, whether they are monarchies, dictatorships, socialistic, or democratic. If they stay within the confines of their ideologies, they can work, but if they stray by one flap of a butterfly's wing, this stability wavers and the system can mutate into something other. Take into account the fates of Tsar Nicholas, King Louis XVI, Benito Mussolini, or Konstantin Chernenko.

Although, on the surface it might seem so, please do not take this piece as a criticism of our capitalistic democracy. After all, this country was built on the backs of capitalists, and they still drive the train. However, by its nature, capitalism creates gaps between the classes, which is not a bad thing as long as they remain more or less constant in size. But when excessive greed causes these gaps to widen unchecked, then wealth and its accompanying power accumulates in the hands of fewer and fewer. At that point, our government of, by, and for, resembles more of an oligarchy.

As with most of life's dealings, the bottom line always comes down to money. It's what drives motives and actions, from the world stage to individuals. Most of the time this works out fine, but when it becomes too dominant, it has the ability to erode trust, faith, honor, love, and curdle the milk of human kindness.

Right now in this country, corporate avarice, as executed by crooks in suits, is going unimpeded. Their transgressions are heartless, for they rarely witness the faces of their victims, thereby mitigating any sense of guilt on their part—if they even feel it at all. But make no mistake; the damage they create is as devastating as any violent crime on the streets. Yet, these felons rarely are caught and even then, are seldom punished.

Some of the biggest players in the Game of Greed are those who have ingrained themselves into our daily lives. First, they ensure their products and services become indispensable, only to pull the rug out from under us. Therefore, let me now present my infamous lineup of Murderers' Row of Greed.

The Good Old Savings and Loan

Batting leadoff, we have the large financial institutions. These sluggers include banks and bankers of all shapes and forms: hedge fund, corporate, personal, investment, international. If it deals with money and its movement, they are a part of this rapacious bunch. Their sleight-of-hand transactions and misdirection of funds give the illusion that all is right in the vaults. However, their recent intentional and reckless tinkering gutted the housing market and destroyed the lives of homeowners, deflated the stock market, and screwed investors and small businesses alike.

Yet, this was only their most recent fiasco. These fine fellows and gals have busted the game many times over the years, trying to control and manipulate financial markets. However, lately, they have become more brazen with the stakes higher than they have ever been and the ever-increasing facility of such acts as more and more money is stored as binary digits.

The harrowing consequence suffered by the guilty parties for all their malfeasance is a monetary fine that amounts to a slap on the wrist compared to the obscene profits their deeds propagated, and the fiscal disaster caused to investors. What's worse, after such a failure, the government-of-the-people bails out these crooks, picks them up and sends them on their merry ways of pranks and follies once again, secure in the knowledge that they are indeed invulnerable and insured against all harm, for being too big to fail. Then, with no remorse whatsoever, they thumb their collective noses at us by increasing fees and lowering savings interest rates smaller than an ant's fart. Then again, what more can you expect from an institution that chains their cheap pens to the desks so you can't walk off with them?

The Drugstore Cowboys

Second spot in the greed lineup is reserved for the drug lords. Not those illicit peddlers, who brandish such intriguing nicknames as Freeway, El Chapo Mexicano, Loco, and The Cocaine Godmother, but rather those legal pharmaceutical manufacturers with monikers like Merck, Pfizer, Roche, and Novartis. These peddlers engage in methods, which should be considered more illegal than those carried out by any of the notorious drug cartels.

As shameful as the banking industry is, these guys are perhaps the cruelest of the lot. On prescription drugs, which cost pennies on the dollar to manufacture, they jack up prices to indecent levels. Please disregard their defensive line of bullshit that the high costs are due to research, development, and testing. Any expenditures incurred by these peddlers are quickly recovered by their ludicrous profits on these medicines. Furthermore, none of their arguments justify the outrageous charges for prescriptions in this country, which cost a fraction as much most elsewhere in the world (the noted exceptions being Antarctica and some remote Pacific islands, where shipping charges will kill you). Certainly, none of their "research and development" vindicates the astronomical price gouging on drugs to treat cancer and other serious illnesses. Many of these medications can easily cost thousands of dollars for each prescription. This has the ignoble effect of forcing many patients to choose between food and other basic essentials or their meds. Many others are driven to cut pills in half to make them last, but diluting their effect. This is the worst kind of greed because of its callousness and the ability to be physically harmful or even fatal.

In some cases, these irreprehensible scum suckers have even hidden the truth about the possible lethal effects of their drugs, choosing to save face over doing no harm. As an example, take the drug Vioxx by Merck, which was used to treat rheumatoid arthritis. The manufacturer concealed questionable test results and manipulated data that showed the drug was responsible for tens of thousands of heart attacks and 38,000 or more deaths. Only after being caught did they admit minimal guilt, and suffered a lawsuit for just fewer than five billion dollars. After legal fees, each claimant was lucky to receive fifty thousand dollars for loss of life or suffering the debilitating effects of the drug's usage. I'm not citing sources for these facts because it's too damn hard to format for this book, and I'm too damn lazy to boot, but you can do an easy internet search and read the sordid facts for yourself. I have no qualms about naming names here, as I was also one of the users of Vioxx for a number of years, and while I have not suffered any noticeable effects as of yet, I don't know what's lurking around the corner for me. The company knew about the risks, but did nothing for years because greed got in their way.

On the rare occasions that these pharmaceutical giants are called out about a particular drug or its high cost, these soulless corporations reduce prices like a jeweler during a sale, thus shedding some insight about their markup strategies. To these greedy bastards I say, grow a conscience and stop screwing around with people's lives. This, of course, will never happen, but at the very least, you can swipe their unchained pens at the doctors' offices.

We Know You Have Many Choices When You Fly…

The many fees charged by our *fiends* at the bank pales beside those of the airplane companies. To name just a few: you have fees for checked bags, unaccompanied minors, flight changes, and frequent fliers. There are seat selection and priority boarding fees. If you make a reservation by phone, you will be charged— go figure that one. If your baggage or your booty is either oversized or overweight, then there is a hefty fee. You'll pay for seat upgrades and not just to first or business class because those have been around since Wilbur charged Orville for that first flight. No, now you will pay to upgrade from economy to something called "premium economy" which buys you a couple of more inches for your bum, more tilt in your recline and perhaps an adjustable headrest. Super, huh? Just don't let it go to your head.

Then there are those insidious charges for amenities, which at one time were included in your ticket price, like meals or snacks, headphones, blankets and pillows. New charges include movie rentals, radio, and Wi-Fi usage. Fees for tray usage, reading lights, blown air, and bathroom privileges cannot be far behind.

When fuel costs were high, the airlines cried distress in order to justify raising prices and fees. Now that the cost of fuel has dropped and their profits are at all-time highs, lowering fares would seem to be in order. Instead, our greedy flyboys have raised prices, decreased the number of flights, and reduced the size of carry-on luggage. They argue they are just making up for lost profits and in the event, fuel prices go up again in the future. Incredibly, they say this with a straight face and all the arrogance they can muster, confident that the public is innately dense enough to believe their garbage.

It wasn't too long ago this country had ten major airline companies, but bankruptcies and mergers have dropped that number down to only four. This simply serves to increase their power and brazen audacity. Recently, the airlines were being investigated for price gouging commuters in the Northeast, who were forced to fly following a fatal train accident which shutdown rail service for several days. One New York City to Washington, D.C. fare went for $2500. When called out on it, the airline muttered something about a mistake being made and reduced the ticket price to around $450. Remarkably, no remorse or moral conscience is shown from these companies, hoping that their ties and smiles will distract you long enough that the stick goes right up your tuckus, which just so happens to be conveniently wedged in the upright position.

Media Blitz

To start with, the cellular phone companies sucker you in with their doublespeak deals, full of Trojan horse offerings, and then they sock-it-to-you when the bills come, which in no way resemble any deal presented to you at the time of purchase. It's been said the devil is in the details, and he most assuredly resides within the incomprehensible pages of these hellish invoices. They are a roll call of taxes and fees for everything from 911 services to compatibility of the phone with your ears. And if you were one of those lucky souls grandfathered in for those obsolete, unlimited data plans, you just might find your download times deliberately slowed down to manage your "excessive" usage. One company now offers rollover data for the unused bytes from the previous month. However, the caveat states you must first use up your current month's allocation before accessing the previously unused data, and at the end of the month, all unused bonus rollovers disappear into the clouds, making it not so much a rollover as it is a tilt.

The mobile phone company's sister conglomerates, the cable and satellite firms demonstrate similar voracious appetites for consumer flesh in their attempt to strangle us with their monopolistic avarice. With only one cable predator in each territory, they are able to write their own checks and usually do so. Any piece of equipment over one coaxial cable into the house is regarded as a la carte, including boxes, modems, and DVRs, all of which come attached with fees that would make even the phone companies blush.

Once they get their fiber optic siphon into you, you will then be presented with a package of television programs strategically designed to convince you to upgrade from their mildly gouging basic cable plan to one of the "Does the Kid Really Need to Go to College?" plans. Thus, ESPN might be bundled with second tier shows such as *Life is Crewel* or *Amish Animal Dentist*, and FX with the *Cooking with Toast* or *Considering Consignments* channels. In essence, this bundling becomes their insurance against you attempting to pare down your monthly bill by removing packages containing shows you would never watch unless you were hanging from a pipe, hands bound, a wet sponge on your head, and live wires attached to your genitals. By ridding yourself of *Planet Zydeco* and *Naked Fat Men on a Raft,* you would also be giving up AE, AMC, and CNN, which just so happen share the same package. You had better believe they got you by the electrodes on this. That's why they're batting cleanup in this lineup.

Oh, and don't think for a second that satellite media services are an alternative, because not only are they cut from the same covetous cloth, but you additionally receive a real attractive dish apparatus to slap onto the side of your home.

The Nation's Grocers

The thing about all these voracious corporations is that they have a tendency to eat one another, growing bigger after each merger meal and hungrier for the next. Whether banks, airlines, media or food companies, their need to feed creates monster firms, too big to nail down when you are wronged by one of them. After feasting at the corporate takeover banquet, the infrastructure of the newly created Giant Corp develops into a hierarchical maze through which your complaints will never emerge.

As a result of all these recent amalgamations, hundreds upon hundreds of well-known and best loved food products in this country are now being produced and distributed by less than a dozen consortiums. Not only have these massive food corporations become less approachable with each new merger, but also they now institute cost-saving measures to help pay for the assimilations, the brunt of which falls squarely on the slender shoulders of the usual victims—the consumers.

After first raising the prices of the goods, their next step is to reduce package or product size. What was once the standard five pounds of sugar now shrinks to four and the traditional pound of coffee slims down to 11.5 ounces and so on. Or sometimes the packaging will remain the same size but include less of the product itself. My very unofficial sources tell me that the current air to potato chips ratio in bags is now around 3:1, down dramatically from the previous 1.5:1 proportion a mere twenty years ago. But the worst insult to consumers is when these companies resort to the ploy of reducing product quality to save bucks, giving us, for example, thinner, more fragile crackers which break even as a knife with peanut butter approaches, or toilet paper dropping plies from two to one.

Criticism is met with unconvincing excuses, which may range from floods in Saudi Arabia to droughts in equatorial rainforests as reasons for pricing increases. Yet, after these natural calamities return to normalcy, cost, size, and product quality remain at the heightened levels. It's hard to know if these companies believe we are all too dull-witted to notice, or we just don't give a scam about what they're doing.

Black Gold

Since the late 1800s, America and the rest of the world have been on the oil standard. Petroleum products either power or create the power that drives mostly everything we do. The vast fortunes it has spawned are infected with their own particular type of greed.

With our environment so maimed and fragile, it's hard to believe we haven't made more use of the many kinds of clean, alternative energy sources available to us. One huge reason is that King Oil keeps its stranglehold on us by refusing to budge from its seat of power. By now, the United States could have been a world leader in green energy, if only the time and money had been allocated, but the oil companies are too entrenched and invested to allow that to happen. They have spent God-awful billions of dollars on petroleum research, drilling, and equipment (rigs, pipes, refineries, tankers, etc.), to switch over to a new platform (pun intended). Therefore, their legion of lobbyists ensures the status quo remains in place. This greed blinds them to the hazy future of our host planet. That is, until the day we run out of fossil fuels or squeeze the last healthy breath out of the atmosphere and oceans.

Baby, You Can Drive My Car...
No, Really, It's Safe. So Go Ahead

Automakers are the folks who rarely, without being forced to that is, let public safety get in the way of greed and profits. It is a fact that on many occasions over the years, car manufacturers have been aware of equipment defects on their vehicles, but instead of spending the money to fix these issues, choose to adopt a "wait-and-see" approach, or even worse, what seems to be an acceptable losses policy. Due to this reluctance to cut into their earnings by alerting the public of possible risks, just how many of us are buckling ourselves unknowingly into a potential time bomb? Many of the car companies refuse to recognize that safety should never take a back seat to dividends, nor moral conscience be considered as an option when lives and heartaches are at stake.

You're in Good Hands?

When it comes to home and auto insurance companies, it seems you're covered until you're not covered. Despite all your protection premiums, you may have a better shot at winning the lottery than collecting on a claim. If you do receive payment, rarely will it cover the full amount of your damages or the replacement value of your loss due to all the riders, exclusions, and acts of God embedded in the microscopic typeset of your contract.

And if the insurance company you're dealing with is not your own, you better hunker down for the long haul. You can expect to experience delays longer than your worse department of motor vehicles nightmare. They'll want their own expert to examine your damage claim, who will be making her prolonged journey by Segway across a certain New Jersey bridge. Additionally, be prepared to receive a laundry list of unreasonable requests for supporting evidence on your claim that will be nothing short of proof of life on other planets. Even after all this, you can anticipate being shortchanged far worse than a notable Manhattan tribe.

*You're Damn Right, This is Not a Bill—
It's the GDP of a Third World Country!*

Kissing cousins with the previous guys are the Health Care Corporations, whose greed you'll find entrenched in red tape and a complicated billing process. They list services you had no idea you received, because you were either under sedation at the time, or the labels for these services were so incomprehensible and insidious as to make even *Gray's Anatomy* of no use.

If you had to undergo an operation, there would be little chance you would be aware of all the doctors who walked into and out of either the operating room or your network. Apparently, that is all that is required to charge for their services—further embellishing your costs.

Health care plans, like any insurance contract, are by nature convoluted and filled with enough muckity-muck jargon to keep you in the dark. You often don't find out you're not covered for a procedure or service until after you've been handed a bill that would have made a nice down payment on your first home. It's not until then that you discover your coverage did not include post-op therapy treatment by the shaman Ngaio Wobutu, and that during the procedure you had been given an infusion of baboon's blood because your plan does not require the more expensive intraspecies blood transfusions. This juxtaposition of the Hippocratic Oath and hypocrisy on behalf of your health care provider may soon result in another medical setback when your suddenly acquired fondness for mutual grooming with others of your breed surfaces. Unfortunately, greed is not a covered expense.

The 1% Plus

At last, there are those individuals in the business *suites* who head these mega-corporations. They are the CEOs, CFOs, COOs, CTOs, etc. whose jobs are to feed the greed machines. They come with salaries, stock options, deferred annuities, incentives, and retirement packages that inflate their pay to more than 300 times that of the average worker. If we're being honest here, who besides Santa Claus or Taylor Swift is worth that kind of money?

Corporate profits are made off the backs of workers (Still with me, Karl?) and from the wallets of the rest of us. The gap between the obscenely wealthy and everyone else grows daily and is, in fact, now more of a chasm than a gap.

There has to be some law in the dismal science of economics, which states that in a capitalistic system, a tipping point exists when a system can no longer sustain itself, when the multitude on the lean side of the chasm can no longer afford the products of those on the pleasantly plump side. What happens then? Hopefully, the well goes dry, and those on the posh side run the risk of dying of thirst, and become fatalities of their own greed.

I'm sure these selfish ones believe they are shielded from this disaster by their wealth. Just like the "myth of climate change," these money mongers assume their green will always provide for them. And that, I'm sad to say, you can take to the bank.

P.S.

Now, lest any of you think I have let our friends, the politicians, off the hook…I intended to include a separate complaint for them in this book. However, after this entire Marxist dialectical diatribe, I'm so done with this gloomy grumble about greed.

Nonetheless, there is no question these legislators deserve a place in this piece as well. Theirs is an exclusive kind of avarice. Yes, some do it for the money, but mostly theirs is a greed for power. If money creates power, then power is what determines where the money comes from, where it goes, and what it does. Regrettably, many politicians end up selling their souls for a few dinners, tickets, junkets, and donations, all cheaply provided by the lobbyists of Big Special Interests. In turn, this endows these politicos with a modicum of power that is dwarfed by the authority they have given away to the soul keepers—the powerbrokers who have purchased the influence over where money goes.

See. I warned you this would be a tale of somber bitching.

Driving Me Crazy

Epistle to the Nomads

It's not that I obsess about driving, because I really don't. On the other hand, it appears I complain a great deal about it while motoring about. It's not me saying this, it's more my wife's evaluation of my on-road behavior. Still, since I do most of the driving, I think I've earned the right to issue my unbiased and technically-sound observations on this matter.

After fifty years of experience on the asphalt jungle, I am all but convinced the art of driving has disintegrated in quality. With so many more drivers on the road today, the statistical probability of acts of lunacy has surely increased. In the interest of honesty and credibility, I will admit that I am not a perfect driver, but I still consider myself a good defensive motorist. When I first started the driving process, I aced the written exam, sailed through the road test, and successfully completed my high school physics course. The importance of this last achievement will become clear a little later on. When I'm behind the wheel, I always practice common sense and try to minimize any distractions, with the possible exception of channel surfing, but even then, I make use of the steering wheel control to flip to my pre-set stations. When my eyesight began to decline, I supplemented it with distance glasses. Then, my night vision took a turn for the worse, and so I learned echolocation, which helped me navigate the darkness. Although I have to admit, fewer people are willing to ride with me now due to the constant chirping sounds.

I believe there are several reasons for the deterioration of driving skills in this country. I'll start by blaming the United States of America; first for its policy of manifest destiny and second for its good old, home-spun, American ingenuity. In the 1800s, the expansionist explosion added a large amount of girth to our country's frame, making it darn near impossible just to stroll to our far borders. After the Louisiana Purchase, the development of the West, and a few parcels of land acquired in skirmishes with Spain and Mexico, we simply had to provide some kind of transportation to get us from sea to shining sea.

To accomplish this, we built the transcontinental railroad, although it probably did more in making some mountebanks from the Union Pacific and U.S. government very rich men than it did to transport folk from here to there. Not long after this travel advancement, the automobile arrived on the scene. Now, no longer track bound, we could go where and when we wanted, that is, when there were some decent roads on which to do this.

American ingenuity gave rise to assembly line production and soon cars were plentiful and affordable, but the roads would remain mediocre until after World War II, when Dwight D. Eisenhower constructed his Interstate Highway System. With the infrastructure now improved, cars not only began to look better, but also came in more sizes and flavors. The family car soon became as indispensable an item as electricity, radios, televisions, and fallout shelters. Yet, this Malthusian explosion of privately owned vehicles soon had the effect of stifling the growth and significance of the mass transit industry in this country to the point where it has been virtually relegated as a third world commodity today.

So, here we are now in the age of personal transportation, where everyone can own a car, due to a glut of used cars, the influx of Asian market vehicles, and creative financing programs which allow buyers to purchase or lease a car for no money down and 1% financing over 946 months or the average American life expectancy. The Union Pacific guys must be toasting each other in their graves on seeing how their progeny continues to flourish today.

Historically, rites of passage have included such things as making your first stone tool, first trip to the agora by yourself, out-swimming the moat monsters, getting your own musket, and sneaking that first cigarette behind the shed. Getting your first car was once a modern rite of passage, but now it seems everyone attains the indispensable automobile upon reaching the age of unreason. Evidently, we don't have enough metal monsters roaming our new roads or inexperienced pilots at their helms.

There are roughly 250 million registered vehicles on the road (Bureau of Transportation, 2011). With that many moving violations out there, the chances of being involved in a traffic accident is merely a matter of metaphysical probability—a random juxtaposition of fate and timing. If this doesn't jostle your concern, compound this with both the substantial size of modern day motor vehicles and the supposed competencies of the other drivers. The bulk alone should strike fear into your crankshaft. Half the vehicles today are larger than the transports used to convey our troops on D-Day, one fourth qualify for their own zip codes, and two specific truck models meet the requirements for statehood. Incidentally, have you ever noticed the bigger the pickup truck, the smaller the head silhouetted in the cab window? If you truly have the urge to operate such a behemoth, then please be considerate enough to ensure there is the proper ratio of gray matter to Chevy Silverado mass.

Of course, there is also the vitally important matter of driver competency. Clearly, we have no way of knowing the skill set of the driver in the other car. This begs the question; does this person possess the ability not to hurt me? Sure, he or she may have a license, but the hardest part of procuring one of those is negotiating the labyrinth of rooms and lines at the Department of Motor Vehicles. After that, all it takes to enter the bumper car arena of life is that small plastic card. And if we're being honest here, the requirements to get hold of one of those are not exactly the stuff of Harvard law exams. All that is needed is to answer a few straightforward questions, such as:

When following a military vehicle carrying weapons-grade plutonium at 50 miles per hour, how far back should you be?

1. *Close enough to read the yellow triangular hazard sign*
2. *Five car lengths behind*
3. *Two state borders away*

So, even if your cranial cabinet possesses something akin to Play-Doh with the spark of a AAA battery, you're good to go on the written part of the test. Consequently, if you grasp the concept of "complete stop" and know the location of a Dunkin'

Donut shop on the road test route, then you pretty much ace the driving part of the examination.

The unfortunate truth is that some people cannot even handle themselves, let alone a two-ton moving mass of mayhem. The scary bottom line here is that much of your safe return home depends on who gets behind the wheels of all those other cars. I hardly have faith in myself in operating a four thousand pound vehicle, and I consider myself somewhere on the hump of the driving skills bell curve. So to put blind trust in strangers driving those other heaps of metal towards me is a wobbly leap of faith at best. After all, the law of averages tells you that many of those other drivers have slid down the backside of that same curve.

In further support of the questionable competency of the other driver, consider this statistic from the National Institute of Mental Health (NIMH, 2005): There are approximately sixty million Americans, 18 years old and up, that suffer from a diagnosable mental disorder in a given year. That creates the possibility that one out of every four cars in this country is being driven by someone with some loose wiring on the old motherboard.

With all these physical and mental obstacles inhibiting one's ability, it should be obvious that driving requires one's full commitment and concentration to arrive safely at the intended destination. Conversely, the car manufacturers have done such a thorough job in equipping the cabin of our vehicles with all the comforts of home that we have become desensitized to the fact that we are even driving. For all the distracting gizmos inside the cars, there are an equal number outside. These might include the many fender benders on the roads, the passing by of attractive members of the opposite sex, those flashing digital billboards and signs, and the rare, but hugely popular, Shriner's tiny-car demolition derby.

In addition to these distractions, there are the many ways a driver's attention can be diverted by multitasking, because Lord knows, driving a car at 40 miles per hour doesn't require our full brain capacity and concentration. Along with the many controls inside the automobile's cockpit, we also have the ubiquitous cell phones, with their chatter and texts; food and coffee with their dripping hotness and messiness; digital music and the necessary manipulation thereof; rogue flaming embers of cigarettes; movies on DVD screens; GPS recalculations; and cranky backseat toddlers. Seriously, can't we just concentrate on the most important task at hand, steering the car with some degree of focus and consciousness? Recently, one newspaper even reported a woman from Ohio, who was obviously such a capable operator that she was spotted driving while talking on her cell phone and breastfeeding her child. That is the honest truth. I did not make that up. I tried, but nothing I could come up with was as good as the real thing.

Driving down the road, with other cars buzzing past me, I am fully aware and terrified that any of these possible distractions could be taking place at that moment. So, for the sake of my sanity, I consciously convince myself that all these other drivers are like me—that is—taking care of business. Subconsciously, however, I am dreadfully pondering which of these distractions, or even an abrupt cough or sneeze, is about to transform this approaching car into a death-seeking missile.

Despite all the bells and whistles car manufacturers slap on their vehicles, driving is still a complicated task; not the actual physical part, such as starting the vehicle, putting it into gear, and then steering. Heck, young children can and have done it. In fact, I'm fairly certain I've even driven behind some of them on occasion. No, the reason it's complicated is that there are two sets of laws governing the art of driving. The first set is one of human administration and would include all the traffic regulations. The second set comes from the laws of natural science—mainly, the principles of physics. Along with the knowledge of both sets of these laws are the two most important standard accessories, which should be in every car, which are common sense and intelligence. Sadly, many drivers view these as options.

The first set of laws should have been learned before one's newly licensed fanny ever sat in the driver's seat. It is required and tested. However, after a period of nervous and cautious driving, many people tend to regard some of these human regulations as less stringent, and eventually, merely as suggestions by the state. All of this is encouraged by a growing confidence and comfort level behind the wheel. The automobile manufacturers' sleek and successful engineering designs make it feel like you're not even on the road, but rather sitting snugly at home in your La-Z-Boy. In the majority of incidences, most people escape serious consequences when fiddling with, cheating on, or even outright scoffing of these man-made laws. Other times, it can result in a fender bender or a traffic citation.

The second set of ordinances, which should not be trifled with or taken lightly in the least, consists of the laws and forces of physics. There is no wiggle room here, folks. They are constant and unforgiving. We're looking at things like mass, acceleration, friction, centrifugal and centripetal forces, gravity, and of course, those three important Newtonian Laws of Motion.

I would like to digress a moment, in order to give a little insight into the amazing Sir Isaac Newton. Although he was one of humanity's most productive geniuses, he was also a bit of a flake, who did some pretty dumb things for such a smart fellow. Granted they were all done with scientific endeavor in mind, but they still lacked the common sense one should have learned as a child. For example, during one of his experiments, just to find out what would happen, mind you, Newton stuck a large bodkin pin between his eye and bone. Fortunately, he wasn't hurt, and with such a trick up his sleeve, he was always a hit at London Royal Society parties. However, kids, if you happen upon a bodkin pin at home, I beg you not to try this. Instead, stick with that thing you do with Mentos and cola. On another occasion of dicey research, Sir Isaac stared at the sun from a dark room with his pupils fully dilated to see what affect it would have on the old orbs. Again, except for having to spend a few days of recovery in a darkened room, he managed to survive his own impetuosity.

Nonetheless, when he was thinking cogently, he did some pretty neat stuff, like the whole gravity thing which would eventually spearhead Albert Einstein's relativity speculations. Much to the dismay of high school seniors, he also developed calculus used to do the work involving time, space, matter, and energy. Then there are his three Laws of Motion, which play such a big part in the art of driving, and the subject of this article.

When driving, there is no escaping these laws of physics. There's no leeway, and no talking your way out of a ticket here.

They are irrefutable, irrepressible, and unequivocal. On the other hand, in their favor, is their reliability. You can count on them to remain constant. For that reason, you know in advance what to expect and can make the necessary adjustments. Nevertheless, you have to know them first, or all is for naught. The main problem is that when driving, far too many people do not think about these laws and forces, or worse, are unaware of their existence. As previously mentioned, driving has become so easy and automatic, even an amoeba could do it if its pseudopod could reach the pedals. With all the new built-in safety features such as airbags, anti-lock brakes, traction control, etc., people drive with a false sense of security, as if they are merely on a ride at the carnival. For this reason, along with learning the traffic regulations, I believe there should also be a mandatory basic course in physics, highlighting Newton's three laws of motion. Therefore, for those of you who did not take the course, or slept through it, here they are in crib-sheet format.

Newton's First Law of Motion

This law is often referred to as the law of inertia, and it states that an object at rest remains at rest, unless acted upon by an unbalanced force. Therefore, your parked Ford Focus will remain so until you get in, start the car, and apply the unbalanced force of its internal combustion engine. Unfortunately, it is in the initial part of this first law where things begin to fall apart. This is because, more often than not, the actual unbalanced force that moves the object at rest is the driver, who is either unaware of both sets of laws (man-made and physical science), drunk, did not opt for the common sense option, or is just tediously dimwitted.

The second part of this law goes on to state that an object in motion continues in motion, with the same speed and in the same direction, unless acted upon by our old friend, the unbalanced force. This might include friction, stepping on the brake, turning the wheel or more emphatically, slamming into the minivan in front of you, of which you had been following much too closely. Other unbalanced forces could include, but are not limited to; trees, brick walls, pedestrians, and alien force fields. Oh…and here's the real kicker with this law…even though the unbalanced force stops your vehicle's motion and speed, you, the driver, will regrettably continue at that same motion and speed until meeting another one of the aforementioned unbalanced forces.

For all the reasons previously mentioned in this article and more, many people simply lose sight of the fact they have two tons of metal, plastic, rubber, and other manufactured particles wrapped around themselves, and when this conglomeration is put into motion, all the formulas kick in. So, at 60 miles per hour, those 4000 pounds of engineering design become a juggernaut, with forces and energy multiplied well beyond my capabilities to mathematically divine.

Newton's Second Law of Motion

Law number two states that acceleration is produced when a force acts on a mass. The greater the mass of the object being accelerated, the greater the amount of force needed to accelerate that object. Simply put, the bigger your car, the more force needed to get it moving down the highway. Thus, SUV owners, this means you will need much more money to pump into the gas tank in order to navigate your Death Star to Walmart, and much more force to push your vehicle out of the ditch you drove into after you flippantly flouted Law One.

Newton's Third Law of Motion

For every action, there is an equal and opposite reaction. This law might be construed as a consequence of the other two laws, if either of these laws is misplayed. So if an accident should occur, then that action will result in an equal and opposite reaction, which could be in the form of fines, expensive repairs, injuries, law suits, jail time, or any combination thereof. Many people quibble that the reaction is not always equal to the action in such cases, but who's to say? Breaking the laws of nature can be a real bitch.

There is a whole kit and caboodle of other physics stuff, which also comes into play when driving. Friction is definitely a major player. Wet, icy, slushy, sandy, and gooey surfaces play havoc with traction. Most people are aware of this and adjust their driving accordingly, but some drivers, who failed the proposed new physics part of the drivers' exam, or simply don't utilize the lick of sense God gave them, still fly over these surfaces as if competing for a spot on the Olympic luge team.

Let's not be mistaken here. It isn't just the speed demons that cause all the problems. Slow drivers present their own set of road hazards. First, as mentioned in a previous complaint, you have the ones who slowly pull from a side road right in front of you, even though the clear path behind your car is as long as the Great Wall of China. This action, of course, causes you to step on your brakes to avoid hitting them. Then to add insult to injury, nine times out of ten, these offending turtles proceed to drive sluggishly, as if they have nowhere special to go, but just had to pull out in front of you to get there.

While I fume over this injustice of motor vehicle courtesy—as I am wont to do according to my wife—the offending intruder continues to move along, one notch above pedestrian speed at best. So slow, in fact, that blowing leaves and tumbleweeds skitter and bounce past my car. In one such instance, there was a Buick in front of me, which couldn't have been doing much more than idling-speed. The next thing I knew, my car was up on blocks, with rims and tires gone, and graffiti sprayed across the car by someone named *RiverWrat*.

Of course, the salt in the wound here is that these dawdlers will make it through any changing traffic lights, while you are stuck behind and watching them chug off. What's more, you then realize that those flickering brake lights you view in distance, signal that you will soon catch up to them by the next block, and your hell-on-earth will continue.

Now, one would think that a multi-lane highway would be the perfect arena for these slowpokes. The far right lane is designated as the travel lane, and anything to the left of it are passing lanes, with the exception of the very far left HOV (high occupancy vehicle) lane reserved for people traveling to Area 51. Therefore, the right travel lane should beckon these creepers like insects to a bug zapper, but what inevitably happens is that some of them spread out into the next passing lane, and yet continue to drive at the same speed as the traffic in the lane they just vacated, with no intention of passing anything. They just park themselves there because they are too lazy to travel in the slow traffic lane, where they would have to deal with oncoming ramp traffic. As a result, they now force everyone else to move over to the second passing lane—if the highway even has one—while they, like plaque, clog up the other two arteries. On occasion, you find yourself boxed in behind one of these slow cars in the travel lane, while a line of clones occupies the passing lane. And you can't do anything but go along with this funeral procession, all the while, regretting you hadn't gone for that exterior option of the tomahawk missile package.

Finally, there are those sloths that make those painfully slow turns. Inevitably, they are always the first ones in line at traffic lights. The light turns green, and the line sits there, while these laggards up front are either, distracted by one of the many things mentioned earlier in this piece, unsure whether they want to take the risk, or are waiting to see what other color options the traffic light has to offer. When they finally do make their turn, they treat it as if it were a family vacation or outing, taking forever to navigate that slow arc, all the while serving drinks, watching the Matrix trilogy, and playing a round of cup-holder golf. Once again, they will be the only ones that will make it through the light, well rested and with many fond memories.

Well, I've covered a lot of ground about driving, and all without the use of a car. Despite my wife's protestations, I believe I have the right to complain about other drivers. After all, my life is in their hands. I have no idea what sort of distraction is having an effect on the attention of the undersized, truck-to-head-ratio driver of the Sierra bearing down on me, who may or may not have failed physics in school, and whose competence and common sense are a crap shoot at best. So today, I think it's best to leave the car in the garage and walk down to the store to get my lottery tickets.

The Final Blessing

"Ignorance is curable; idiocy is chronic."

- Anonymous

That about does it. Now, aren't you glad you came along for the ride? Of course, these epistles do not represent all I have to complain about. I'm quite certain I've forgotten a few that will come to me later. Then I'll mutter to myself, "Damn! I should have included this one or that one. How could I have forgotten those doozies?" And, I'll still wake up most days to find new things that boil my stew. Still, I believe I've covered most of my prized possessions.

I'd like it to be known that, despite all my grumblings, most of the time I'm not really the Donny Downer portrayed within these pages. It's only when read together like this that I come off making Ebenezer Scrooge look like Jimmy Carter. Moreover, I believe this to be true for most curmudgeons. We are not constantly complaining, because in doing so, we would be diluting the importance of our messages and increase the likelihood of not being taken seriously. A true curmudgeon tempers his or her protests to preserve credibility and thus avoid becoming a social turnoff like the misanthrope, who couldn't give a shit anyway.

Personally, I can't help myself when it involves carping about something I view as wrong. I wasn't far from serious when I claimed a genetic proclivity towards curmudgeonliness. I recall my father griping a lot to family, relatives, and especially the television. His beefs were usually accompanied by, what I referred to as, "the two-handed salute," which could occur either before or after the pronunciation of his grievance. To do this, Dad would fling his arms up in the "surrender" stance and immediately throw them forward to a horizontal position with the hands flopping downwards as emphasis. This gesture of disapproval might be followed by a verbal utterance, best described as either "awwww!" or "sheessh!" depending on his level of disgust. Recently, many people close to me have claimed to have witnessed me making a similar salute and they were quick—much too quick to my way of thinking—in pointing this out.

While I know it is not the most pleasant circumstance being around someone who grumps and gripes a lot, sometimes you need a person, such as me, if only to allow the rest of you to keep a proper perspective on reality. For obvious reasons, you cannot keep frustration bottled up until something breaks in there. So if you are one of those people who cannot spout off yourself, due to either your upbringing or a temperament fostered by genetic inclination, then let us professionals do the dirty work for you. Perhaps, just by hearing us find fault with things, it will relieve some hidden stress you have accumulated over time. And maybe, just maybe, you will begin to feel a little better. After all, you didn't break your vow of possessing a good nature by openly criticizing something. We did it for you and then went on our miserable ways.

However, just be careful not to absorb too much of our vitriol at the risk of your turning down the wrong path and becoming one of us. Because the truth is, we need you guys to stay true to your patient dispositions. For you are the yin to our yang, the positive to our negative, the north to our south, and the jumbo to our shrimp. After all, this is what makes the world go round— this and that whole conservation of angular momentum thing. We wouldn't know what to complain about if your kind didn't show us what is right, and you people wouldn't know how good you have it, unless we pointed out the bad.

But if you ever do feel the need to carp, go out and find something to rag on, or feel free simply to borrow one of mine. Give it a good airing and see how it feels. If you're not accustomed to spewing protests, just give it a minute or two to sink in. After doing this, you will notice a sensation of joyous conviction and relief flood over you. And whether the irritating itch is scratched or not, you will still have experienced the curmudgeon catharsis that keeps us going—that sense of satisfaction that in some small way you did your part to right the wrongs of the world, or at least those of the pinhead up the street. Who could ask for more than that?

While I still grit my teeth, curse out loud, and pound the steering wheel over perceived outrageous acts of insensitivity and moral injustice, it sure did feel good—at least for a while—to get some of this off my chest. That is, until tomorrow, when some idjit will most certainly do something stupid to goad my good nature. Until then I remain,

Irascibly yours,
The Curmudgeon